Celebrating the Fourth

D1498391

Celebrating the Fourth

Ideas and Inspiration for Teachers of Grade Four

Joan Servis

Foreword by Regie Routman

HEINEMANN
Portsmouth, NH

Heinemann
A division of Reed Elsevier Inc.
361 Hanover Street
Portsmouth, NH 03801–3912
www.heinemann.com

Offices and agents throughout the world

The author and publisher wish to thank those who have generously given permission to reprint borrowed material:

Figure 6–2 from *Mathland: Journeys through Mathematics: Daily Tune-Ups 2* by Julie Pier Brodie et al. Copyright © 1996. Published by Creative Publications. Reprinted by permission of the publisher.

Figure 8–1 © 1995 *Student-Led Conferences* by Janet Millar Grant, Barbara Heffler, Kadri Mereweather. Published by Pembroke Publishers and available from Stenhouse Publishers, 1-800-988-9812.

"I am asking you to come back home" from *Stories I Ain't Told Nobody Yet* by Jo Carson. Copyright © 1989 by Jo Carson. Reprinted by permission of the publisher, Orchard Books, New York.

Library of Congress Cataloging-in-Publication Data
Servis, Joan.
    Celebrating the fourth : ideas and inspiration for teachers of grade four / Joan Servis : foreword by Regie Routman.
      p. cm.
    Includes bibliographical references and index.
    ISBN 0–325–00145–6
    1. Fourth grade (Education)—United States. I. Title.
LB1571 4th.S47   1999
372.24'2—dc21   99-27311
                            CIP

Editor: Ray Coutu
Production: Vicki Kasabian
Cover design: Michael Leary Design
Cover photo/author photo: Donna Terek
Manufacturing: Louise Richardson

Printed in the United States of America on acid-free paper
03 02 01 00 99 RRD 1 2 3 4 5

To my husband, Jim,
my closest friend

Contents

Foreword

Regie Routman

Joan Servis and I have been close friends and colleagues for more than twenty years. We met when we were both trying to figure out how to make teaching more memorable and meaningful for ourselves and our students. Over the years, we have continued to share teaching stories and family stories, good times and hard times, teaching goals and life goals.

Joan writes like she talks and acts—with common sense, energy, passion, and humor. Reading *Celebrating the Fourth* is like going on a journey with a good friend and coming home recharged and invigorated. Joan tells us how and why she continues to rethink and change her practice, work with her colleagues, and guide students to make responsible choices for their behaviors in all areas of the curriculum.

One of Joan's greatest strengths is that she knows how to make every member of the classroom and school community feel welcome and valued—beginning on the first day of school. She understands the developmental characteristics and abilities of nine-year-olds, and she capitalizes on their interests and sense of humor. She keeps pets in her classroom, tells jokes (that her kids laugh at), encourages her students to bring their favorite collections to school, and holds classroom meetings to establish procedures and solve problems that affect everyone. She treats students fairly, respectfully, and honestly. She fosters independence and encourages self-discipline. She models how to resolve conflicts through peer mediation, how to develop organizational skills, and how to get along well with others.

Joan expects the best from her students, and she gets it. She takes students' suggestions for getting things done in the classroom and gives them lots of responsibilities and choices—where they can sit, what jobs need to be filled and who will fill them, how to create bulletin boards, what rules the class will follow. How do her students act so responsibly, even when she's not in the room? "I build community," Joan says. "I share control and have high expectations that students will practice self-control. I trust them and encourage them."

The wonderful community Joan establishes extends to her students' families. She invites parents to visit, to share their talents, and to help out in the classroom. In her first meeting with parents in the fall, Joan entertains them with stories about her life and family while encouraging them to tell their life stories to their own children. She tells parents what she loves about fourth graders—and their children in particular. She expresses her hopes and goals for her students, answers parent questions, and ends by reading an inspiring poem. She hands parents the required curriculum information (to read on their own), which also describes her philosophy, goals, and homework expectations. Joan's actions with parents reflect exactly how she teaches her students: by first engaging them personally and by respecting and valuing them, students eagerly seek to learn and become an integral part of the classroom community.

Joan invites us into her literacy-rich classroom and demonstrates how she sets up the room, organizes for teaching, teaches minilessons, individualizes instruction, gives homework, assesses, deals with required curriculum and grading, and sparks enthusiasm for learning. In reading, she demonstrates how she values choice, uses reading logs, employs formal and informal assessments as well as conducts student self-assessments. In writing, she shows us how she establishes a writing workshop in which her kids not only learn to write well but to love writing. In math, she describes how students problem solve in small groups using manipulatives and working together. In science and social studies, she builds in student choice on a mandated topic and teaches students to gather information, take notes, and present their findings—often through simulations and role playing. She also presents, in great detail, how she and her students prepare for student-led conferences—creating a time line, establishing a conference agenda, organizing portfolios, rehearsing for the conference and preparing parents, and setting manageable goals with both the teacher and parents.

Joan Servis is one of the best teachers I have ever known. It's not just because she teaches well and deeply; it's that she inspires her students to learn confidently and to continue to love learning. In this terrific book, we see how she celebrates and learns from all members of the community—students, teachers, parents, and administrators. While she gives lots of suggestions for being professional and to improve our teaching, it's through her own example that we learn her secrets.

Teachers have always known—or quickly find out—that without a smooth-running classroom, you can't teach much. Kids need to feel safe, valued, and respected before they can learn. Joan Servis teaches us how to create an environ-ment that makes kids feel important. At the same time, she makes teaching rig-orous, keeps expectations high and realistic, and helps students make wise choices. *Celebrating the Fourth* is a must-read for every intermediate-grade teacher who has ever struggled with and thought about changing her teaching. You will laugh out loud, admire the honesty, welcome the humility, and treasure all the practical suggestions. You will be a better and more thoughtful teacher for having read and savored this remarkable book.

Acknowledgments

I wrote this book because of my colleague Regie Routman. She encouraged me to write down what happens in my classroom, convincing me that my experiences would interest other educators. Her support through letters, phone calls, and coffee chats, and her suggestions after reading my rough drafts were crucial. I love her, thank her, and hold her in the greatest esteem as my mentor and friend.

I am honored to be associated with Heinemann. My thanks to the hardworking members of Heinemann's staff. My greatest appreciation goes to my editor, Ray Coutu. With his assistance I improved my writing. He supported and cheered me. Because of our many conversations he has become a close friend.

In the beginning, Toby Gordon believed I could write this book. Mike Gibbons gave me suggestions, books to read, and encouragement. Vicki Kasabian guided me through the production process, patiently answering my questions.

I want to thank the following friends for taking the time to read my rough drafts and giving me suggestions:

Julie Beers, who stretches my thinking. Her daily offerings of love and creative ideas kept me energized throughout the entire process; Linda Cooper, an energetic colleague whose enthusiasm for learning and teaching inspires me to be a better teacher; Kristi Roberts, a reflective teammate willing to sit and talk about teaching. Her willingness to do more than her share, always with a beautiful smile, makes teaming with her a joy; Helena Servis, my loving cousin, who was supportive and insightful when I needed help; Anika Simpson, a fourth-grade teammate, who asked challenging questions; Diane Siska, a fourth-grade teacher who gave me valuable insight into what teachers want to know. Her enthusiasm sustained me in my struggle to give practical help to teachers; Thelma Tucker, former teacher and close friend of many years, whose intellectual and reflective nature encouraged me to rethink my ideas; Deedra Uth, a caring neighbor who makes me feel special, especially when she brings me bags of her delicious homemade cookies; Judy Wells, district math consultant, who was willing to take time out of her day to talk with me about my math chapter; and Rosemary Weltman, my former principal, a source of inspiration, who has given me the courage to put my actions into words.

A special thanks to Fred Bolden, a fourth-grade teacher whose talent with computers is extraordinary, and who was always available with technical assistance.

I am grateful for my family, my son Mark and his wife, Nancy, my daughter Marie and her husband, Dale Fowler, my stepfather, Shoukry Khalil, and my husband's mother, Mina, for their love and encouragement. My five grandsons, Daniel, Ryan, Luke, Kyle, and Nathan, have provided me with smiles and kisses. I needed them.

My husband, Jim, deserves a medal. With infinite patience he put my entire manuscript on the computer. Without him I would still be trying to finish this book. The amazing part is he still loves me.

I would also like to thank my colleagues at Onaway Elementary School. I appreciate having their support and friendship and the benefit of their expertise. Most important, I am thankful to my fourth-grade students, past and present. Their joy and enthusiasm have made this book possible—and necessary.

Introduction

There Is No Ceiling in Our Room

The head custodian at my school loves to tell everyone that I have been teaching as long as he's been alive. What keeps me going? Like the Energizer Bunny in TV commercials, I keep getting "recharged" by my fourth graders, nine-year-olds going on nineteen, bringing stuffed animals to school, yet worrying about the loss of the rain forest in South and Central America. It's a truly magical age: hugs one minute, arguments the next. Our classroom is a bustling place full of chatter and laughter. I like being there, and so do the students. But it wasn't always like this.

In the Beginning

I did not go into education because I had a burning desire to teach. I selected the education track because women in the fifties did not have many alternatives. I could be either a nurse or a teacher. Because I faint at the sight of blood, I chose teaching. You might say I became a teacher by default. I never dreamed I'd spend so many years in the classroom or enjoy it so much.

My own elementary education was very fragmented. My father was in the Air Force, which meant we moved frequently. I attended schools in Michigan, Virginia, Texas, and California. I always found it difficult not to talk to friends in class or get out of my seat. Not surprisingly, I spent hours in the office of Mrs. Thornquist, the principal of Santa Monica Elementary School. She informed me that I was one of the top ten "problem" children in the school, but I didn't mind being released from the tedious lecturing of the classroom teacher. Being restless and bored as a child has given me, as an adult, a keen sensitivity to students with similar problems.

When I began my teaching career, good students were obedient and quiet. For almost twenty years I was a "skill-and-drill" teacher, dutifully following the teaching manuals—and wishing I was in some other profession. My husband would ask me why I kept teaching. I'd answer, "Because I have long summer vacations to spend with my two children."

Why Did I Start to Change?

I did not have a teaching philosophy that I could articulate. My attitude was "Follow the manual." I never reflected on how children learn best or why I did what I did in the classroom. I never watched anyone else teach. When I ate lunch in the teachers' lounge, my colleagues and I discussed the behavior problems of difficult students. I spent hours grading papers and wishing students invested more of themselves in their work. Sometimes I thought I was the only one who cared about assignments.

In the early eighties two things happened that caused me to reflect on my teaching practices. Regie Routman, our basic skills tutor, who was conducting research for *Transitions: From Literature to Literacy* (1988), pointed out the watered-down version of Roald Dahl's *James and the Giant Peach* in our fourth-grade basal reader. She encouraged me to obtain multiple copies of Dahl's book. She also started slipping copies of professional articles into my mailbox, which challenged me to rethink my practices.

Eager to eliminate the boredom in my reading class, I bought or borrowed copies of *James and the Giant Peach*. For the first time, my students and I got excited about reading. Because I didn't have a manual, I did what most teachers would do: I "basalized" the book, creating dittos with endless questions. Still, reading the authentic text was a vast improvement. It gave me the confidence to put aside the manuals and trust in my own judgment. I read widely in the professional literature, I questioned my procedures, and I developed a personal philosophy about how students learn best. I had started on my journey toward becoming a different kind of teacher, one whose philosophical stance is based on the belief that learning should be authentic, meaningful, social, reflective, and sensitive to students. It is fortunate that I teach in Shaker Heights, a progressive district that encourages teachers to experiment with new ideas, because I was able to explore and change without fear of criticism from the administration.

My Struggles with Change

Initially, I struggled with the issue of control. I did not think students could be trusted to select their own writing topics or their own books for independent reading. Reluctantly, I stopped giving "story starters" and adopted Nancie Atwell's writing workshop approach.

Luckily, largely through Regie Routman's initiative, we had a teacher support group, which met weekly at noon. We were a small group of about five teachers of third through fifth grades who gathered to talk about the changes we were making in our classrooms. Our experience ranged from beginner to teacher of many years. I could not have continued my own journey of growth and change without that group. We were all struggling to implement the writing workshop and to introduce a literature-based approach to reading. We were honest with one another about what worked and what didn't. We recommended books and articles we found helpful. We observed each other's teaching during our planning periods. We discussed educational theory and how to put it into practice. I had always worked in isolation. Now, for the first time, I was involved with a group of teachers all sharing their expertise.

Frank Smith's book, *Joining the Literacy Club*, helped me to question what I was asking students to do. Were my assignments purposeful? What did *I* do as a reader and a writer? Did the students *see* me as a reader and a writer? Slowly I began to open up to my students. When they read during Sustained Silent Reading, I did too. At first I found it hard to resist grading assignments or tackling the paperwork on my desk while students were engaged. But as I started to see myself as a model, I opened a book and joined in.

I began to observe my students' reactions to the assignments I gave them. Nancie Atwell stresses the importance of letting students select their own writing topics, but I wasn't convinced. I decided to use literature as a model for writing and chose Judith Viorst's delightful *Alexander and the Terrible, Horrible, No Good, Very Bad Day*. After reading the book aloud to my students and brainstorming about our own "horrible" days, I asked students to write about their horrible day. Most of the results were brief and poorly written. Then I realized that, even though I was using literature, I was still giving story starters. Students had little choice and didn't really care about the topic. Once I began to reflect, observe, and ask students for their ideas we became collaborators. Slowly, things changed.

What I Believe

Today I articulate my philosophy of learning in a handout for parents, which I distribute at the beginning of the school year.

I believe

- all children are capable and can be trusted to learn.
- in collaborating with students in planning curriculum activities.
- connections are necessary between students' daily lives and the curriculum to give authenticity to assignments.
- daily self-reflection and assessment are vital for students and teachers.

- learning is social, and thus conversation and teamwork in the classroom are necessary.
- in creating a classroom environment that encourages risk taking.
- in giving students choices with responsibility for their decisions.
- students should have access to everything in the room so they feel ownership of their environment.
- in heterogeneous grouping for math and reading.
- in demonstrating how to do written assignments and in providing models.
- what is done in the classroom lays the groundwork for lifetime skills and habits.
- it is important to applaud successes daily, celebrating the positive and diminishing children's fear of failure.

What I believe drives what I do. Sometimes I unconsciously revert back to how I was schooled. I don't always act rationally, and I sometimes *react* emotionally. But when I make mistakes, I try to be kind to myself. The next day I start afresh and strive to do my best. In *Interwoven Conversations: Learning and Teaching Through Critical Reflection*, Judith Newman says, "Teaching is a daunting job. The best job we can ever do is just try" (1991, 213).

How I Am Still Changing

Change is not easy. It involves a continuing process of looking, listening, reading, and reflecting. It is discomforting and can even be threatening. As teachers, most of us have been taught to think of ourselves as the purveyors of knowledge. It goes against our long-held beliefs to ask students to be part of the learning process. I find it difficult to listen to students question or criticize my carefully planned lessons, to hear their honest responses. But my willingness to change the way I teach has benefited all of us. There is no ceiling in our room. Students can soar—and they do!

Why This Book?

The purpose of this book is to urge you to reflect on your own role as a teacher. I want you to discover how exciting the classroom can be and to cheer on your efforts. In the chapters that follow, I write about what I do in my classroom. I want you to see that my enthusiasm for teaching has everything to do with attitude, a willingness to change and collaborate, and much less to do with expertise. I am an ordinary individual who has found a way to encourage and draw on my students' talents. My classroom is now our classroom. Together, my fourth graders and I are becoming a community of learners.

1

What Do I Know About Fourth Graders?

I began my career in 1960 teaching kindergarten. I had a hard time because I couldn't play the piano or sing on key, so my students learned songs to the wrong tunes. Two years later I moved on to first grade but lasted only a short time. The first-grade kids couldn't seem to stay with a topic for more than five minutes. Second graders worried about everything and took things much too seriously. Third grade was a vast improvement due to the students' longer attention span, but when I landed in fourth grade, in 1977, I finally felt at home.

I am fortunate to live and teach in Shaker Heights, Ohio, a suburban community diverse in race and in levels of education and income. The population of our school district includes 5,634 K–12 students. According to the 1997–98 District Annual Report, the racial breakdown is 43 percent white, 51.2 percent African American, 2.9 percent Asian, 0.7 percent Hispanic, and 2.2 percent multiracial. More than 90 percent of Shaker Heights students go on to college. Classroom size is, on average, twenty-four students, classrooms have adequate supplies, and school functions are well attended. For the most part, students receive the resources and the services necessary to meet their needs. I teach at Onaway Elementary School, a K–4 school with 470 students. I am aware that not all schools are so well funded and serviced; I have worked in poor rural and large city districts and never cease to appreciate the fact that I can focus on what happens inside the classroom.

No two children are the same, and it is difficult to predict with certainty what any child will do. Like the rules of the English language, there are always exceptions. Just when I presume to know what the fourth graders are thinking, I am taken completely by surprise. One year, after teaching what I thought was a stimulating curriculum, I received a thank-you note from one student's mother, which said, "Rob told me his favorite thing was watching you open your Christmas presents." It was a humbling experience and has helped me avoid taking myself too seriously ever since.

Over the years, however, I have observed some common traits, and I draw on these commonalities in designing developmentally appropriate lessons that support and encourage student success.

They Work Hard

For children, fourth grade marks a big leap academically. Students are expected to be independent. Learning requires more abstract thinking. Content areas, such as social studies and science, demand more time. Most of my students seem to enjoy school and respond well to the heavier demands, but every year I encounter students who would rather be anywhere else. At the end of one school day, two boys got into a fight over who would be first in line to leave the building. I asked them why it mattered. They told me they each wanted to be first out because they hated school!

Most nine-year-olds, however, are enthusiastic and curious. They like to be busy and respond well to active, project-based learning, but they rarely know how to manage their time wisely. One of my jobs as teacher is to help students develop organizational skills. In September I tell them, "By the end of this school year you will be organized." I want them to know that organization is something we all need to learn.

A project is an in-depth study of a topic lasting three or four weeks. During our study of plants and animals from various ecological communities, or biomes, the students read to gather information, took notes, wrote a paper, and created a clay model of a desert plant and animal. With others researching the same biome they presented skits to the class. When I tell parents in the fall that students will work on most projects in class, they applaud. They have spent too many late nights helping a child who has waited until the last minute. At school, I can offer help by creating a time line to keep track of their progress.

The resources needed for research are already in the classroom. I can direct students to information, support their interests, talk with them about the next step, connect them to other students or adults who can help them, and bring in videos and speakers to supplement the topic. When students complete a project under a teacher's guidance, they can follow the process. Fourth graders are willing to work hard when the goal is well defined and the directions are clear.

They Have Individual Differences

I pay careful attention to students' individual differences and to their personal likes and dislikes. Children are more likely to succeed when they are intrinsically interested in what they are doing. Aaron, for example, hated fiction but was a voracious reader of books about World War II and former presidents. When I assigned a biography as a long-term project, he selected John Kennedy. I encouraged his interests and did not force him to read fiction for his self-selected reading.

Aaron wrote letters to famous people during writing workshop and received autographs and photos in return. His classmates were intrigued. Aaron hated working in a group and was considered opinionated, but he began to make an effort to cooperate as he became recognized as someone who had knowledge worth sharing. I referred to him as our class expert on World War II and presidents. We drew on his expertise.

Aaron worked hard and became happier and more confident. If I had forced Aaron to read fiction, I am sure we both would have been miserable. I don't read fantasy or science fiction. Does it matter? I always try to decide what aspects of the curriculum should be negotiable. I am encouraged by the words of Curt Dudley-Marling, a professor who took a year's leave from his university to teach third grade: "What is important to remember is that, if students do not use reading and writing in school to fulfill their intentions, they may not discover the power of reading and writing to affect their lives." He goes on to say, "Permitting students to bring themselves and their lives into the classrooms is, I believe, a moral imperative" (1995, 11–12, 14). I agree. I can encourage children to broaden their interests, but I have to be willing to give them control, to let them express their personal and cultural identities. It is a delicate balance.

They Value Friendships

"Children of this age tend to be interested in almost anything that concerns their friends—what TV programs they watch, how early they have to go to bed, or how much they have to help around the house," say Dr. Louise Bates Ames and Carol Chase Haber of the Gesell Institute of Human Development (1990, 28–29). Students gladly help each other. They love to work in pairs, so I permit them to choose partners. Those partnerships often turn into friendships.

Friendships frequently last throughout the school year. They are usually based on common interests and rarely cross gender lines. A nine-year-old's happiness is evident when he or she has a close friend. Kayla and Elaine, both overweight and unpopular, became fast friends. Whenever there was a choice of partner and in most classroom social situations, they were together. I was glad they became close pals because the other girls usually did not include them in their group at lunch or recess.

Friendships can help to bolster academic skills as well. Amber, a bright student who viewed herself as my classroom assistant, was a close friend of Cherie, a student with a multitude of learning problems. Cherie did not pay attention to directions, had difficulty reading, and rarely did her homework. Amber came from a home that stressed education and supported her progress at school. Cherie was not so fortunate. Her mother did not come to conferences. In fact she visited the school only twice during the year, once for the end-of-the-year program.

Amber was a model for Cherie and encouraged her to complete assignments. The two of them would frequently include Joyce, another classmate, in activities, such as working on maps and projects. Joyce had difficulty making and keeping friends because she was so intense and anxious. Amber and Cherie's friendship provided a level of comfort for all three girls. It's easier to be inclusive when you feel good about the world.

They Love to Collect Things

In *Your Nine-Year-Old*, Ames and Haber (1990) note that "Nines love to collect. Not only quantity but quality is now important. And he likes to keep his collections in order. His success in collecting is in part due to his persistence and his desire to accomplish a goal" (5). Since persistence is a trait I encourage, I am glad it can be nourished by the nine-year-old's natural interest in collections.

Every student in my class has several collections, which might include baseball, football, and basketball cards, Beanie Babies, stuffed animals, miniature china animals, stamps, dolls, coins, and toy horses. A collection gives students a personal identity. My students love to bring their collections to school, and I find this a good way to build community. They are interested in each other's collections and the stories behind them. And sharing collections allows every child to feel a sense of belonging, even the child who has difficulty getting along.

Long-term friendships can begin with common interests. My son, who collected reptiles, developed a very close friendship with Ron, also a reptile collector. They spent hours together, poring over books and discovering information about these animals and their care. The bond they formed still exists today, twenty-seven years later.

Whenever possible I turn to collections as a starting point for writing. Roberto and Bronson wrote a self-published book entitled *A Book for Collectors of Baseball Cards*. Each chapter told about a certain aspect of collecting cards, such as how to determine value, where to sell cards, and so on. When they shared their book during writing workshop, the others asked, How many cards do you have? What is that card worth?, which led to lengthy discussions about their own collections.

They Respond to Humor

When people ask me what I like about fourth graders, I say, "They laugh at my jokes." Nine-year-olds have a wonderful sense of humor. They love to laugh.

While reading a recent issue of "Responsive Classroom," a newsletter for teachers published by Northeast Foundation for Children, I identified with a comment made by a Massachusetts teacher: "Having a good sense of humor helps when teaching fourth grade. We're dealing with a lot of serious issues. It's important to be able to inject humor at opportune moments to relieve the tension."

I tell lots of funny stories about myself and my family. Recently, I told my class about my five-year-old grandson, who lost his temper when I told him he was a sore loser. He said, "Shut up, Grandma!"

"Oooohhh," murmured the entire class.

I described how I reprimanded him. "Kyle, you can't tell Grandma to shut up. You must show respect to Grandma. You will apologize!"

Folding his arms, sticking out his lower lip, he replied, "No way, José."

The class roared! We spent ten minutes sharing similar incidents with "annoying and naughty" younger siblings.

During writing workshop some students regularly employ humor. The class applauds and laughs at their articles, stories, and letters, encouraging these playful authors. In a letter to future fourth-grade students, for example, Eli wrote, "One thing that I am sure of is you will like the 'Smart Pills.' They make you smart and only the highly skilled teachers know how to make the formula. They look like Skittles and they are made in Mrs. Servis' basement where she keeps the formula (S_1, K_3, I_2, T_4, T_3, L_6, E_2, S_1)." I always pass out Skittles to students before a test, telling them the S printed on the candy stands for "smart."

I like to read aloud funny books, such as *There's a Tarantula in My Purse and 172 Other Wild Pets* by Jean Craighead George. The book is made up of short stories about the humorous antics of wild animals living in the George home. It inspires my students to recall funny incidents about pets in their own homes and balances the seriousness of our learning with a little levity.

They Like to Talk Things Over

I'm a sympathetic listener—to a point. Because fourth graders tend to complain a lot, I try to keep their behavior in perspective. They get especially flustered when faced with an unpleasant situation or task. Harlan, for example, sulked for days because his mother forced him to join the noon Junior Great Book Club, a group that meets weekly to discuss literature. Harlan preferred to play outside with his buddies.

Ames and Haber (1990) say, "Nines are likely to growl, mutter, sulk, or find fault if things don't go well" (42). With a sense of humor, a few words of assurance, a sympathetic but firm response, however, I find that complaints often dissipate. This year when I had the students draw names for science partners, some of the male-female pairs grumbled, so I said, "You're not marrying them. You're only working as their partner in science for six weeks." Everyone laughed and accepted the situation without resentment.

If the whole class complains, I take time to listen. Sometimes it is important to resolve the problem immediately. At one point, for example, the students were unhappy with their art class. They felt they did not have enough time for drawing and painting. "She talks half the class. . . . We can't get started until the class is almost over. . . . We don't have enough time to work on our pictures."

It is not my responsibility to tell another teacher how to do her job, so I approached this colleague with extreme care and sensitivity. "The students are asking for more time to work on their artistic activities. I'm certainly not questioning your procedures, but I wanted to let you know about their concerns, so you can explain why you need to instruct them so much at the beginning of class." I knew that if the art teacher shared the rationale behind her methods, the students would at least have the opportunity to tell her about their concerns and would not feel so powerless, even if they didn't agree with her.

Children feel better if they are allowed to express their feelings. If I've been away from school for a day or more, I often hear from the entire class about a substitute teacher. The most common complaint is, "She gave too many directions." Most nine-year-olds don't like to be given unnecessary directions. They feel insulted. I always try to request substitutes I know my students like.

A disruptive classmate can become a cause of widespread grumbling. I always tell students to state their complaints in writing and post them on the message board. Their words are private because the notes are stapled shut. I promise to respond. One note read:

Dear Mrs. Servis,

Jeff is insane, rude, and has terrible manners. I dearly hope you take our concerns in deep consideration. Remove him. I tell you remove him.

Your students,
Aalayah, Mike, and Rachel

I met with Aalayah, Mike, and Rachel to get more details. The trio objected to Jeff's unkind remarks, his refusal to cooperate or work in a team, and the piles of books he stacked on the table they shared. I then met with Jeff privately and talked with him about having more consideration for his neighbors. I asked him to talk with his table mates about resolving the problem. I was in fact asking the entire group to use conflict resolution, which we practice at our school in the form of peer mediation (described further in Chapter 3).

Finding solutions to situations involving disruptive students is a challenge. I never know where to seat them. Is it fair to ask calm children to put up with a disruptive one? I haven't found perfect answers, but I've tried a variety of approaches. When the child in question is absent, I enlist the help of the rest of the class. In *Beyond Discipline*, Alfie Kohn (1996) says, "The best choice for dealing with problems, or for preventing their occurrence in the first place, is to involve the support and ideas of the community" (115). We shouldn't pretend "we" don't have a problem. Because nine-year-olds are naturally eager to help, they will often volunteer to sit next to a problem child. They will take it on as a cause. We talk about the importance of modeling the behavior we want the disruptive student to emulate.

Early in the year, Mark, a child with a reputation as a troublemaker, got into a serious altercation while I was away for the birth of my fifth grandson. When I returned to school, I discovered that his punishment, administered by the principal, was "in-house suspension." While he was serving his time, I called a class meeting.

"Ladies and gentlemen, I need help. Mark has some habits he needs to change. As you know, he is at this very moment sitting in the office, unable to be part of our class. I feel bad about this. I'm sure you do too, and I'm even more sure that Mark feels worse than any of us! How can we help him?"

"I think he behaves like he does to get attention," said Jessica.

"Maybe we should try to ignore him," added India.

"We should not laugh at him when he acts up, and maybe he'll stop," chimed in Roberto.

At this point I complimented the students on their mature analysis of the problem. "I agree with you that Mark likes the attention he gets when he acts up. He's probably been doing this in previous grades, and it has become his way of behaving."

Dave volunteered, "I'll sit by him, and he'll see me doing my work and paying attention."

"So you'd be a model of good behavior for him?"

"Yes. I won't laugh at him. I'll show him how to be real nice."

"I notice he always is playing with something," said Robbie, "and I have a rubber eraser he could use to keep his hands busy."

"That's a wonderful idea, because he does need something quiet in his hands. I think your ideas are very helpful. Is anyone else willing to sit near Mark and demonstrate good behavior?" I asked.

"I can't handle sitting by him," interjected Erica. Several other students agreed that they too would have great difficulty sitting next to Mark. I appreciated their honesty. The class decided that Mark's table should have only four students, Mark and three others who were positive they could influence him through their own behavior. No one ever suggested punitive measures.

We concluded by discussing how a good student behaves and the necessity for the entire class to listen to instructions, complete tasks, and allow others to focus on their work. We agreed not to laugh at Mark's attention-getting antics.

The seating switch happened immediately. The volunteers were excited about being "change agents." When Mark returned to class I told him privately that the students at his table chose to sit with him to help him stay on task and that he could keep his hands occupied with Robbie's rubber eraser if it did not leave his possession. Mark reacted positively, pleased that these students wanted to be his friends. As the year progressed, his behavior improved, assisted further by his close friendship with Andrew, a serious student.

They Demand Fairness

"Nothing is fair to the nine-year-old who is also struggling with the cognitive task of understanding ethical behavior at a new level," says Chip Wood (1997), author of *Yardsticks: Children in the Classroom, Ages 4–14*. Fourth graders do not want to be blamed for something they didn't do. Determining who started an argument is important to them. I don't say, "I don't care who started it. You're just as bad if you're involved," because that results in sulky, resentful children. I can stop the dispute, but I can't solve the problem. The parties involved can usually find a solution if they are given the opportunity.

I go out of my way to hear both sides of an argument. I ask children to describe how they are feeling and what they would like their opponent to do. Often this is enough, and the two parties apologize and shake hands.

I never punish the entire class for the misdeeds of a few. The unfairness of that tactic upsets fourth graders immensely. A frequent topic when we gather together to discuss problems is unfair treatment in the past. "We had to all stay in at recess just because a couple of students were acting up. . . . The lights were turned out in the lunchroom and we all had to put our heads down. I wasn't doing anything wrong. . . . The sub took minutes away from our free time and I was being good! It's not fair." Fourth graders have a strong desire for justice.

In *Punished by Rewards*, Alfie Kohn (1993) says, "Punishment also provokes resistance and resentment, which a child may take out on other people, such as peers. It leads children to feel worse about themselves since they often assume they must be bad if someone keeps doing such bad things to them. And it spoils the relationship between the child and the adult: a parent or teacher who relies on punishment becomes, in the eyes of the child, a rule enforcer, someone who may cause unpleasant things to happen—in short, someone to be avoided" (167). I learned this again recently when Kristen, a student of mine from fifteen years ago, told her mother that I had unfairly accused her of disturbing others when she was in my class. She has never forgotten it.

They Are Honest

Most nine-year-olds are truthful. They rarely lie to adults. Instead, they offer excuses. In fact, two of my students, Robby and Dave, wrote a book entitled *Twenty Excuses for Not Doing Your Homework*. Another student, Jessica, wrote one entitled *Twenty-five Excuses for Being Tardy*. All three polled the class for excuses they would use. Here are some of them:

For not doing homework:
- My mother threw it away.
- I wasn't home.
- My baby brother tore it up.
- My baby sister scribbled all over it.
- It fell in the toilet.
- My dog peed on it.

For being tardy:
- Our clocks stopped.
- I had to feed the dog.
- The bus forgot to stop at my corner.
- I thought it was Saturday.

I don't entertain negative theories about the motives of children. I believe deep down that children are honest. I assume children will behave virtuously, and they do. In our classroom, we don't lock up things of value and I haven't had a serious problem for years. If an object is missing, the students start looking everywhere, and it usually turns up. Ames and Haber (1990) corroborate my experience: "Nines rarely take things that don't belong to them, and if they do they want to return them to set things right. They are now developing a sense of ethical standards and they mean to live up to them" (50).

We did once have a problem when desserts began to disappear from lunches. The students confided to me that they had a suspect. There was a great deal of interest in the "crime." I moved the lunch baskets from the hall into the classroom and asked the students to keep an eye on them. We had no further problem. The child the others suspected had a problem with being truthful, and I discussed this gently with her parents.

The Buck Stops Here

In *The Portable Pediatrician's Guide to Kids*, Dr. Laura Nathanson (1996) says, "If you're a nine through eleven kid, your relationship with the teacher is more complicated than before. How you feel about the teacher can make a big difference in how you learn" (211). In my classroom, the student is at the center of the learning process. As a teacher, I attempt to recognize individual needs and build on individual strengths according to each child's developmental progress. It is part of my job to consider the developmental abilities and characteristics of my fourth graders when we come together as a community of learners.

Dr. Nathanson adds, "If you feel like a teacher is your friend, you feel that you can take risks and even if you fail, he or she will still like you" (211). I try to remember that taking the time to nurture caring relationships has academic benefits. What a joy to have so many friends in one room.

2

Community Building

Despite many years of teaching, every fall I am overwhelmed. There is so much to do. Administrators want completed forms, tutors need my schedule, and the weather never cooperates. It's always hot. Wasps fly in and out of our unscreened windows. Students' attention span is short. I find myself longing for those summer afternoon naps (Why, I ask myself, did I choose this career when I could have worked at a desk in a quiet air-conditioned office somewhere?). But, despite the physical discomfort, excitement is in the air. On the first day, an eager group of students sits expectantly, clutching book bags filled with new spiral notebooks, pencils, markers, and other school supplies. Their eyes survey the room as they await instructions on how to begin.

To new teachers, my advice is "Build a community within the first six weeks." In *Life in a Crowded Place* (1992), Ralph Peterson says, "Bringing students together as a group and nurturing tolerance for their ways and beliefs while celebrating their differences challenges the talents of the most experienced teachers. Teachers who make communities with their students are cultural engineers of sorts" (13). Here's how I begin.

Long before the first day of school, I lay the groundwork for the year by ensuring that the physical environment is welcoming and interesting.

Creating a Home Away from Home

Recently, I moved into a new classroom. As I faced the stacks of boxes, the furniture crammed into every corner, the four empty bulletin boards, and the piles of books on every table, I had the sinking feeling that moving had been a big mistake. But then I reminded myself that I moved to be closer to Julie Beers, another fourth-grade teacher, with whom I wanted to collaborate.

I toyed with the idea of leaving everything the way it was. When the students arrived I'd simply tell them they were in for some major physical labor. But I didn't have the courage to welcome students to a classroom in total disarray, even though it certainly would have been an adventure. Arranging the room could have given them a strong sense of ownership, but I like order. I was unwilling to jeopardize a smooth beginning.

So I began unpacking boxes and putting things away, keeping community in mind. I arranged the room to encourage collaboration, creating places where we could gather in large and small groups: a space on the rug for sitting together to promote discussion and sharing; comfortable chairs, colorful curtains on the windows, and large pillows on the floor to give the classroom a homey feeling; tables (instead of desks) to encourage conversation and group work. On the tables I placed baskets of pens, pencils, markers, highlighters, and colored pencils. Sharing these writing tools would help to establish a mood of cooperation.

Some years ago, Regie Routman convinced me to eliminate the teacher's desk to help convey the idea that the classroom is child-centered. I found it difficult at first. Where would I put my lesson plan book? Where would the student teacher and I pile office memos and handouts? I have compromised by using a small table that is not, as my desk was, the first thing you notice when you enter the classroom.

Students bring a favorite mug from home to hang on the wall, and once a week we drink juice from our mugs while reading the newspaper or the newsletter "Time for Kids." Crates and bookcases offer books for browsing and reading. One long bookcase holds individual mailboxes where students can keep their clipboards and books. The room also has three computers, a television, and a VCR.

I told my students I wanted them to think of the classroom as their "home away from home." Scott blurted out, "There's just one more thing I need in order for this to be *my* home away from home!"

"And what is that, Scott?"

"My fish tank."

Classroom pets add a great deal to the climate of caring. Institutions such as hospitals and nursing homes often allow pets, as regular visitors or residents, because of their positive benefits for patients. I've always tried to bring lots of animals in the classroom. Recently I received a letter from a former student, just married, telling me that he and his wife were contemplating the purchase of a guinea pig because of his special memories of the one in our fourth-grade classroom.

Although I arrange the classroom to promote collaboration, the students and I often make changes later. When the class complained about congestion at the

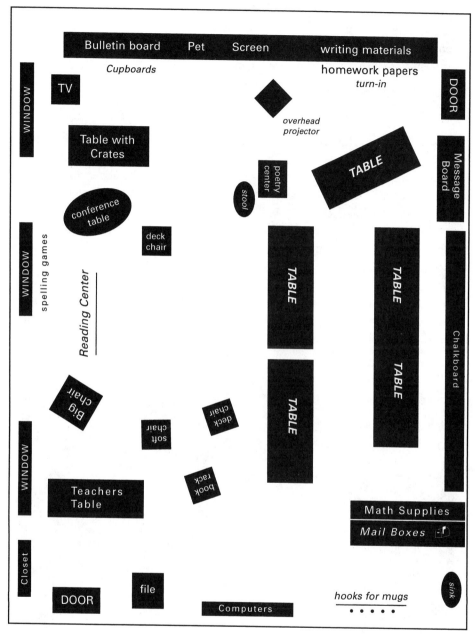

Figure 2–1. Classroom Layout

mailboxes, I relocated them. When we found ourselves crowded on the rug, we moved a table to create more room. The physical layout of the classroom should encourage talking together, allow access to supplies, and provide ease of movement from one place to another (see Figure 2–1).

Creating Bulletin Boards

Years ago I noticed that children weren't paying much attention to my bulletin boards. Now I ask my students to design and arrange displays. I don't like teacher-made boards anymore, because I regard children's work as more attractive and interesting. Displaying children's work again sends the message that ours is a child-centered classroom.

Although I don't create the bulletin board displays, I do think about them over the summer and usually designate one or two for specific purposes. One always serves as a message board, accessible to everyone all year. It is constantly changing as daily notices, articles, notes, and news clippings are added and removed. The others are blank, except for the colorful backing I put up before the first day, ready for students to fill up as needed. When my colleague Julie moved to fourth grade, she told me that her former third graders loved looking at their

Figure 2–2. Fourth-grade self-portraits

self-portraits all year, so we borrowed mirrors from the art room and did our self-portraits (see Figure 2–2).

Leslie Bakkila, a former fourth-grade teacher in our district, shared her idea for creating an alphabet of mathematical terms: "Aa is for angle," "Gg is for graphing," and so on, and this list now forms the basis of our first math lessons. David M. Schwartz's book *G Is for Googol: A Math Alphabet Book* (1998) is an invaluable aid in this activity (see Figure 2–3).

Sometimes I ask for volunteers to design a bulletin board as a special project. We meet together to talk about possible themes. The students sketch a plan for my approval, then create the board. Examples of past boards include graphs of favorite foods, subjects, and books, which tied in with our unit on data. The students interact more with bulletin boards they create. The boards also help them feel that the room belongs to them.

Regie Routman sums up my feelings when she says, "By giving students some ownership of the bulletin boards, they take more pride and responsibility for how the room looks and functions" (1991, 426).

Figure 2–3. An alphabet of mathematical terms

Having prepared the physical environment, I turn to the social environment when the students arrive.

Getting Acquainted

On the first day, I always devote lots of time to getting acquainted. We gather on the rug and introduce ourselves. We share our names, where we are from, and something special about ourselves. Last year I told my class that my oldest grandson, Daniel, was their age. I am a grandma. Nine-year-olds love their grandmas. Immediately, we connect. I continue to point out connections.

"Maggie! My grandma's name was Maggie, so your name is very special to me," I might say.

"Lisa Marie, my daughter's name is Marie, so I will always remember your middle name."

"Matt, I had your sister, Jessica. I would have been disappointed if you were not put in my class."

"Mary is very special, class. She has a famous sister, Sarah, who was my student the year Mrs. Routman's book *Invitations* was published" (I hold up the book). "And Sarah is famous, because she is on the cover, here, in pink. Do you see the family resemblance? This was my class on the cover." Mary is beaming.

Personal comments like these set a friendly tone. We begin to know each other. Before school begins, I scan my class list for familiar names, looking for siblings of my former students and thinking about possible comments. I am reminded of what Dorothy Watson, a professor of education at the University of Missouri-Columbia, says in "Welcome to Our Wonderful School": "Building community takes time and talk" (Watson 1996, 283).

Introducing the standard first-day information blitz in a light manner lets my class know I'm a teacher with a sense of humor. I laugh a lot, which helps my students warm up to me. I agree wholeheartedly with Ralph Peterson (1992): "Teachers can encourage a playful spirit by expressing themselves joyfully, engaging in exaggerated and playful gestures, being ready to give new interpretations to the mundane, and taking delight in original expression" (58).

I might say, "I know what is most important to you. I know what every one of you is sitting there wondering about. You want to know, When do we eat lunch?"

"Yes," says the class in a chorus.

"And you want to know, When is recess?"

"Yes!"

"And, When do we have art and physical education?"

"Yes!" they all shout.

By this time we are all laughing. I tell them about about lunch, recess, and special classes. Then I ask, "What have you heard about homework in my class?"

"No homework after Memorial Day," several students answer in unison.

"Right. And you want to know if that's true again this year?"

"Yes."

"Well, I believe in traditions. Families celebrate them, and we will become like a family, working and playing together all year. We must carry on the tradition. There will be no homework after Memorial Day."

"Yeah!" cheers the class.

The entire scene resembles a pep rally. Parents often tell me at the fall social, an annual picnic on the lawn the second week of school, that the first thing they heard from their children was that there is no homework after Memorial Day. It's a big deal.

Connecting with Books

Four years ago, my school district provided a weeklong workshop led by Shelley Harwayne, the author of *Lasting Impressions* and the principal of the Manhattan New School, an innovative public elementary school in New York City. She recommended devoting big blocks of time in September to language and literature. I follow her advice. I like to read aloud lots of picture books and short stories with an eye toward making personal connections. On the first day I usually read something by Robert Munsch, a Canadian author, whose colorful illustrated books are short and humorous, and feature repetitive phrases that prompt students to join in.

"I love Robert Munsch books," I tell them. "Have you heard of him? Most people know *Love You Forever*, but if I read that to you I'll cry." That really grabs their interest. A teacher who cries is a real person. "I don't want to cry the first day of school. So, I'll begin by reading another Robert Munsch book called *Mortimer*. You can join in anytime you think you know what is coming next." The pattern is so predictable, students love to read parts of this book with me. We can usually be heard way down the hall.

I also encourage students to bring their own favorite picture book to school and read it aloud to the rest of us, another good way to make connections. Students often like perennial favorites. One year, for example, I was amazed to discover Kim's most beloved picture book was the Little Golden Book by Janette Sebring Lowrey, *Pokey Little Puppy*. I must have read that book to my daughter, Marie, a hundred times when she was little (see Figure 2–4).

Even parents get involved. They visit the classroom, gather the students around them, and read a favorite picture book aloud. I invite other teachers, the principal, custodians, and secretaries to share special books with our class

Figure 2–4. Glynae reads her favorite picture book to the class

too. Our classroom community reaches out to the larger school community. Coming together as readers helps us all feel closer and leads to satisfying conversations.

Me Boxes

"Me Boxes" are another way I build community early in the year. My students and I fill small cardboard boxes, usually decorated, with small objects that say a lot about us. The first week of school I bring in my Me Box and share each item with the students. This year my Me Box contained

- a bookmark about Robert Louis Stevenson, which represents my love of reading and my favorite childhood poet
- a small iron horse, which symbolizes my childhood collection of miniature animals as well as my love of horses

- my University of Michigan lapel button, which tells them I graduated from the University of Michigan—and have season tickets to all home football games
- a note card to illustrate the hours I spend writing letters and notes to family and friends
- a picture of my previous class, because I'm a teacher
- CDs of Beethoven and Tony Bennett to show that I like classical music and that Bennett is my favorite singer
- photos of my husband, children, and grandsons to signify how important my family is to me
- a membership card for the Nature Conservancy to represent my interest in preserving the environment
- my cat calendar symbolizing my love of cats

By modeling how to choose and talk about a Me Box, I help students get to know me while giving them ideas about what to include in their own. In a letter to parents, I describe the idea behind the Me Boxes and set a deadline for their

Figure 2–5. Kindergarten pal shares "Me Box" with fourth grader

completion. After we have shared our boxes with each other, we share them with this year's kindergarten pals in Susan Mears' class. Fourth graders become models for many activities. The kindergartners, in turn, share their Me Boxes with us (see Figure 2–5). This year we learned that Matt is interested in sound effects in films, Hannah hikes the White Mountains with her family, Bakari loves basketball and has won several trophies, Elena collects artifacts representing her Hispanic background, and Betsy performed in the musical *Showboat*.

When Michelle Raeder, our student teacher, brought in her Me Box, students were very interested in its content:

- pictures of her two sons, Troy and Adam, currently in middle school
- a calculator representing a tool from her former job in business
- a book, *Lost World*, symbolizing her love of reading
- her wedding picture
- her college graduation picture
- published works by her sons from elementary school showing her interest in writing
- baseball tickets to illustrate that she likes sports

In those few minutes, Michelle showed us what she loves and values, and we all felt closer to her.

Establishing Rules with Students

On the first day of class, I am always tempted to go over all the procedures and rules that make the classroom run smoothly—such as when to sharpen pencils, when to use the bathroom pass, and when to go to hall lockers. But this is boring stuff. Students remember only half of what I tell them. Instead, I am guided by Alfie Kohn (1996): "Each aspect of life in a classroom offers an invitation to think about what decisions might be turned over to students or negotiated with students individually and collectively" (85). I don't simply tell students about procedure, we establish them together.

I ask what kind of classroom we want. Students always request a peaceful environment. They want to be able to do their work without lots of noise and distractions. We brainstorm about the rules that would foster this kind of classroom. Because my students sit at tables in groups of four or five, I ask them to talk together and make a list of the rules they think we need and state them in a positive way, for example, "We will be responsible for our own materials" rather than "Do not leave your things all over the table."

After the groups have developed their lists, we join together as a whole class and review their suggestions. I give them my reactions and sometimes question a shortsighted rule. When one group suggested the rule "Raise your hand when you want to speak," for example, I asked the students if there were ever times when we didn't raise our hands. We talked about literature discussion groups and math and science groups, and suddenly we had a long list of occasions when raising our hands made no sense. Even the students couldn't come up with a good reason for the rule; it was simply a holdover from the past. As a teacher, I see how easy it is to fall into that trap of adopting procedures without considering them carefully first. We changed it to "Show respect for the person talking." We agreed that someone should be able to finish what he or she has to say without being interrupted.

The time invested in these discussions pays off because students view the rules as "ours." Power struggles virtually vanish. Students who rebel against rules ("Nobody tells me what to do") are more cooperative if they have a say.

We draw up a final list of rules and post them somewhere in the room. Here is a sample:

Classroom Rules
1. Show respect for the person talking.
2. Be responsible for your own materials.
3. Practice self-control.
4. Use conflict resolution (peer mediation language).
5. Use quiet voices.

Establishing Basic Routines

Some daily routines need preliminary discussion to minimize conflict and other problems.

Bathroom Privileges

Since I need to know where all students are at all times, I do not negotiate the bathroom privilege. But I do ask students when they need to go, to take the pass, a pink and blue feather duster, from a hook and return it when they come back. I always make a great show of demonstrating how to dust the bookshelves on the way to the bathroom (I've actually seen some children do it). Once I used pink and blue toilet bowl brushes (in case, I said, students got the cleaning urge). Well, one fourth grader actually returned to class with a dripping-wet brush and announced "I cleaned the toilet." Stories like these keep us all from being too serious.

Pencil Sharpening

A good problem-solving activity during the first week is the question of when to sharpen pencils. I ask small groups of students to think about when to sharpen pencils and if there are exceptions to those times. After each group has listed and discussed their thoughts, we come together. Usually, the students are stricter than I would ever be: "No pencil sharpening after the bell rings."

Because pencil sharpening doesn't bother me unless I'm talking to the entire class, I tend to view the student reactions as extreme, but I know teachers who can't stand it at all during the day. When I tell the students that I don't mind pencil sharpening, they relax their guidelines. I also keep a supply of sharpened pencils on hand, which students can use at any time to reduce unnecessary trips to the sharpener.

Locker Assignments

For years I had complained about our twenties-era coatrooms designed for smaller students, thinner coats, and no book bags. So I was thrilled to discover that my new classroom had lockers directly outside in the hall, just like middle and high school. Before assigning lockers to the new fourth graders, I talked about how hard habits are to break, how we sometimes prefer the familiar. Then I announced that students who had been assigned lockers in previous years had the option of keeping those lockers. It's important to be sensitive to issues like this, which may seem minor to us but are major to fourth graders.

These preliminary activities help us to get acquainted as a class and prepare for what we will do together in the classroom throughout the year.

Classroom Jobs

Members of a family pitch in to help with household chores. The same willingness to participate builds community in the classroom. I do not assign classroom jobs. Instead, the students and I talk about how people donate time in Shaker Heights. I mention that I volunteer for responsibilities as a staff member in my building. We are happier when we have choices; allowing students to choose jobs is an easy way to foster happiness in the classroom.

The first week of school I ask the class to list the routine tasks that need doing so our classroom runs smoothly. The list usually includes washing chalkboards, running errands, and watering plants. I add a few more, and we wind up with Tub Toters (people who carry tubs filled with lunch bags to the lunchroom), Forecaster (a person who writes the daily schedule on the board, which, like the weather, may change), Librarian, Gofer (errand runner), Poet (a person who daily reads poetry aloud to the class), Chalkboard Washer, Overhead Cleaner, and Phone (a person who answers the classroom telephone).

The jobs are entered along the top of an 8-by-11-inch sheet of paper, which is passed around for sign up, and a weekly rotation begins. I record the week the student performs the job after each name (see Figure 2–6).

Some chores, such as Gofer (which provides an excuse to visit another location), are popular. Washing the overhead transparencies and hanging them on the clothesline to dry ususally has a shorter list of names, but I have never ended up with a job unfilled.

Students become experts at tasks they enjoy. Dan, for example, took his role as Librarian very seriously. Every day, he read out the names of students with overdue books or fines, requesting that the books and the money be turned in to

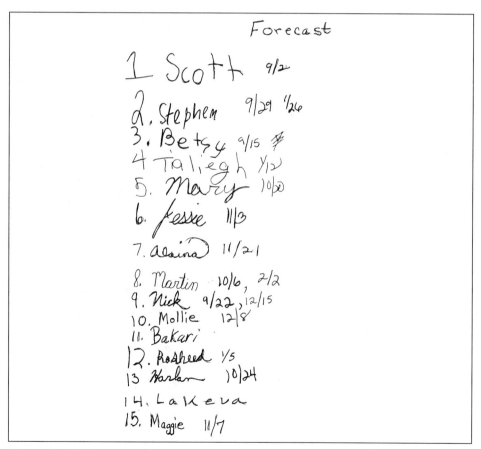

Figure 2–6. Job sign-up sheet

27

him so he could bring them to the library. Reading names aloud is very effective, since it puts pressure on the offenders. Because of the efforts of students like Dan, our overdue list is practically nil, which makes our school librarian happy and gives the job holder a feeling of accomplishment. I agree with Ralph Peterson (1992): "Jobs help students contribute to the quality of life in the learning community as well as negotiate meaning, take on responsibility, and contribute in significant ways to advancing a cooperative way of life" (63).

Being a Model

According to Alfie Kohn (1996), "teachers who are not part of a collaborative network of educators find it difficult to help students work together" (110). I try to be an active member of the adult community at my school. I sign up to serve breakfast to our staff. I eat lunch regularly in the staff lunchroom, mingling with colleagues from all grades. I provide treats at staff birthday celebrations. I write thank-you notes to secretaries, custodians, and other teachers when they do something nice for me. I run in and out of my colleague Julie Beers' room and vice versa, sharing ideas and getting help. Students see this and learn from it. In an October pen-pal letter Hannah wrote, "I'm new to Onaway. I moved from Massachusetts and to Onaway. My pal is Dinah and she's in Ms. Beers' class (I'm in Mrs. Servis') but Ms. Beers and Mrs. Servis are *good* buddies and their classroom has a door that connects to our classroom. We leave the door open because Ms. Beers is always popping in (sometimes just to say Hi)."

I seize every opportunity to show my students that I am a caring person. In the fall, when former students often visit the classroom, I stop everything to give hugs and make introductions. I want my current fourth graders to know that relationships forged in the classroom can last forever.

Making Celebrations a Priority

Steven Levy, the author of *Starting from Scratch* (1996) and a master teacher, reminds teachers, "Celebration builds community and we don't do enough of it in our classrooms" (170).

Every day we applaud small successes and happy events—a well-written lead in a piece of writing, a lovely pencil sketch, a poem read with great expression, announcements read over the PA, the birth of baby brothers and sisters, and other similar happenings. I am always looking for opportunities to evoke a warm family feeling.

To celebrate small successes, I write congratulary notes to students and attach them to the message bulletin board. I send postcards to parents to make them aware of their child's positive behavior or academic success. They tell me how important these postcards are, that they're often more meaningful than any other communication that's ever been sent home from school. Sometimes I take notes in class when I see a child do something his or her parent would be interested in knowing about. I like to be specific because every parent feels his child is special. To help me focus on all my students, I keep a record of each note or card.

One of the perks of teaching for many years is hearing about the successes of former students. I welcome every opportunity to share these successes with my current fourth graders. Recently, at the bank, I ran into Donald, who is now a successful dentist. I told the students how proud I was because Donald had been very naughty and I was pleased he had "channeled his energy in a positive manner." I also invite former students to talk about their experiences with my class; Matt described his trip to Australia and his year of living with an Australian family. I ascribe to the words of Ralph Peterson (1992): "Celebration is perhaps our finest way of caring for others. There is a selflessness that is expressed through celebration. The other person is the focus of our attention, and we are one with them as we celebrate" (45).

Does community building take time away from instruction? Certainly, but it is well worth it. When the classroom becomes a community, children want to come to school. It's like being part of a family. We tolerate our idiosyncrasies, celebrate our differences, and applaud our achievements.

3

Fostering Independence

In February 1997, I received a phone call from Susan Berg, the manager of training programs for a company providing human resource services. Through one of my students, she had heard about my interactive way of teaching students, encouraging them to apply knowledge in new situations, and wanted to visit and observe. Susan explained that training classes at her company were taught through lectures, and students didn't apply what they learned to problems. We set a date for her visit and she spent three days with us, inconspicuously taking notes.

Thinking back on Susan's visit, I realized that I want every student to have the confidence, self-discipline, and skills to function without constant direction from me. Over the years I've discovered that fourth graders are capable of doing more than adults—including me—permit. By working in groups and searching out answers for themselves, my students gradually become more independent. What are some of the things I do that help them achieve this independence?

Being Sensitive to Student Concerns

Independence thrives in a climate of acceptance and mutual respect. As the teacher, I care about my students and demonstrate my concern for them, their problems, and their feelings. As a result, my students are able to express their ideas comfortably.

Discussing problems makes us more sensitive to the needs and feelings of others. At the beginning of the year, I take Alfie Kohn's (1996) suggestion and ask students, "What makes school awful sometimes? Try to remember an experience during a previous year when you felt bad about yourself, or about everyone else, and you couldn't wait for the year to be over. What exactly was going on when you were feeling that way?" (114).

The incidents students report are not, in my view, big problems, but I try to be sensitive to them nonetheless.

"I had to be perfect."
"The teacher yelled at me."
"I had to memorize poetry daily."
"I got behind and I never caught up."
"We never got recess."
"A few students ruined the class, because they were bad and upset the teacher."
"I was teased for being short."
"The day is going great and then someone calls me a name and the day is ruined."
"Other students knocked down the structures I built. I had spent lots of time building them."

When problems arise that affect everyone, we hold class meetings. Following the guidelines Kohn outlines in *Beyond Discipline* I meet with students to talk, plan, or reflect on behavior problems. These meetings often reveal underlying social dynamics. In the fall everyone participated readily except for three boys. In fact, these boys were causing some of the problems we were bringing to the circle. They mocked other students and were unfriendly to everyone but each other. I felt frustrated by their refusal to join in. When I prodded one of them, Harlan, into revealing how he felt when he was teased about being skinny, he laughed and acted the clown. The class responded with laughter. I asked the students not to laugh at Harlan, since he was laughing out of discomfort.

In retrospect, I think I was wrong to prod Harlan, since student participation in circle meetings is voluntary. He was not ready to share so early in the year. I need to be patient and wait, even though I have the power to "force" an issue. Fortunately, as Harlan became comfortable in our classroom, he began to make friends with other students. Sometimes I forget that building a community takes time.

Class meetings take time, but the mutual respect and caring they encourage are worth every minute. The process is ongoing, however, and I have to remind myself that name calling and unkind comments will not stop simply because I hold a classroom meeting. Scott made fun of Elena the day after a session in which we discussed problems associated with teasing. I said to him, "Where were you yesterday when we talked about how hurt we are when we are teased?"

Trusting Students

Another necessary part of fostering independence is trust. I trust my students and I tell them so. But it is not enough to say, "I trust you." I have to back up my statements with actions that demonstrate trust.

Regie Routman describes one way I express trust in *Literacy at the Crossroads*. I don't require students to record the number of pages they read each evening in their self-selected books. I expect my students to complete their nightly reading. Asking them to log pages doesn't motivate them to read and since creating lifetime readers is my goal, I have dispensed with this time-consuming process.

Not all my colleagues agree. Some feel it is necessary to hold students accountable. When I point out that I don't record the number of pages I read daily, they argue that I am an adult and don't have to prove I'm reading. But Judith Newman says in *Interwoven Conversations* that we should err on the side of expecting the best of people, rather than policing everyone. I only ask my students to record the title of their books when they finish, as I do. It's a matter of trust.

Using Students' Ideas

Adopting students' suggestions for better ways of doing things gives them a sense of ownership. By "ownership," I mean having some control over your own literacy and learning. I use students' ideas. In fact, I ask for them. As our community develops, students become vocal about improvements and alternative ways of implementing curriculum. Our curriculum is dictated by state and district curriculum guides and courses of study, but how it is implemented is entirely up to the teacher and, in my case, to the students.

I am not alone. Julie Beers' fourth-grade class was negotiating everything with her early in the school year. Due to looping (moving from one grade to another, class intact), the class had developed into a close-knit community of learners in third grade and felt secure in speaking out about how things should be done.

After producing their September newsletter for parents, Julie's students asked for a larger role in the next one. "You did way too much this time, Ms. Beers." As the deadline for the October newsletter approached, Julie suggested having every table work on one page. The students said, "That's a terrible idea, Ms. Beers." They wanted to do exactly what they had done for the September newsletter, which was for each one to write an article. They also suggested that they do all the illustrations, graphics, and cartoons. "We don't want you to do any of that!"

Julie jokingly said to me, "Sometimes I think they're too comfortable with me." Because she is eager for her students to be independent, Julie was able to relinquish more of her role in producing the newsletter.

Giving students lots of choices in every area, academic and social, helps them feel invested in what is happening in the classroom. For example, I allow my students to have some control over where they sit, since changing seats is a simple way to make them happy. I initiate a switch once a month, honoring particular requests whenever possible.

I might say, "Class, we're going to make some seat changes today. My only request is that our classroom reflect our neighborhood and the diversity Shaker Heights represents." The groups represent a diversity of race and gender, but there are exceptions. If the class is not evenly balanced, it may be necessary to have an all-male or all-female table.

"Now, who would like to change seats? Maggie, I'll let you go first because I received a note from you on the message board requesting a seat change a week ago. Who would like to change seats with Maggie?"

Three or four hands go up in the air. Maggie makes her selection, which puts her at a new table with a different view of the classroom.

I ask the class who else wants a seat change and continue to let students choose from volunteers. After about fifteen minutes, I say, "That's all for today, but if you'd like a new view of the classroom why don't you shuffle your seats around at your table?" Usually four or five students rearrange themselves, giving everyone the satisfaction of having made a change.

Gender can be a big issue in fourth-grade seat changes. When Mollie ended up at an all-boy table, she was crushed. She scurried around the room trying to make other arrangements. Likewise, Martin wound up at an all-girl table, and he was sulking. He tends to withdraw when he is upset, and I noted his unhappiness. I suggested that Mollie and Martin exchange seats, even though it created an all-girl table and an all-boy table. Their feelings merited an exception to our usual criteria. Both were happy to change seats.

Julie Beers also hears from her students about seating, but organizes it differently. She asks students to list on a card two boys and two girls they would like to sit next to and promises they will get to be alongside at least one person they put on the card. Then she makes up a seating chart. Fourth graders think the process is fair and never complain.

It takes time to develop the kind of risk-taking atmosphere that encourages students to express their wishes, ideas, and opinions, and to act on them without constantly consulting me. In the beginning of the year, students ask me many unnecessary questions: "May I use my mug to get a drink of water?" "May I go to my locker?" "May I bring my Beanie Baby to school?" My response is always, "If it does not interfere with your learning."

As the year progresses the questions become more thoughtful and less procedural. For example, when we were revising our student-led conference agenda (described in Chapter 8), the students objected to my request for a two-week sweep of their independent reading. A "two-week sweep" means maintaining a log of the self-selected books they read over a two-week period and recording the number of pages they have read every day. The purpose is to give a sample of what students accomplish in independent reading over a specific period, thus enabling teachers to make some generalizations about each student's progress. It is an assessment tool many teachers use in our school district.

The students asked, "Why do we have to mark down what we read for two weeks? Sometimes I'm reading the same book for two weeks because it is very thick." After a discussion, the students overwhelmingly decided to cross it off the agenda. They felt that their reading logs, a record of the books they have completed, achieved the same purpose and could be shared with their parents.

Giving Students Responsibilities of Their Own

Students will never be independent unless they assume responsibility. For years I have espoused the credo "Never do anything for the students they can do for themselves." The moment they walk in the door, my students are responsible for copying down from the overhead projector our "Things to Do" list, which includes all the flyers, newsletters, and announcements that parents need to read. It also lists homework assignments. Students gather all the necessary materials and attach everything to their individual clipboard along with the "Things to Do" list. Then they put the clipboards in their mailboxes and take them home at the end of the day. Every evening they clear the clipboard; the only things that come back to school the next day are completed assignments and the "Things to Do" sheet. This system prevents papers from being lost at the bottom of a book bag or looking like they've been crushed in a blender. In newsletters, I frequently remind parents to check the clipboard every evening instead of asking their children if they have homework. Sometimes I write notes to parents on the "Things to Do" list if a child has a problem turning in homework or I have any concern relating to behavior (see Figure 3–1).

Every week we read our "Time for Kids" newsletter and drink juice. The students receive a rotating schedule for providing juice. Each week, a different student brings in three cans of frozen concentrate, mixes them in the pitchers provided, and serves the class. If a student forgets, we don't have juice. Consequences.

Name: _Jessie_

THINGS TO DO

	FINISHED ☑
Monday: 11/3	
1 Web - finish book for interview	☐
2 Math - "Convince Me" Word Problem	☐
3 Reading Questions in Spiral	☐
4 Flyer for Parents	☐
5 Vote Tomorrow	☐
6	☐
Tuesday: 11/4	
1 Election Day	☐
2 Estimation ditto	☐
3 PTO Shirt sale tomorrow	☐
4 Biome bird materials	☐
5 Web	☐
6	☐
Wednesday: 11/5	
1 Conferences next week	☐
2 Web	☐
3 Math Page 105 Textbook	☐
4 Reading - finish biome book	☐
5 Flyer	☐
6	☐

Figure 3–1. Things to Do

The students are also in charge of their March conferences with parents (described in detail in Chapter 8). There is massive preparation for these conferences as students sort their completed work, organize, and practice. Sarah, reflecting on how a conference went, said, "It made me feel responsible." Similarly, during reading discussion groups (described in Chapter 5) students are responsible for leading the discussion, thus developing leadership skills (see Figure 3–2).

Another avenue for encouraging independence is peer mediation. For seven years, Julie Beers and I have been recruiting fourth graders, training them, and implementing a peer-mediation program. Peer mediators work as teams to help students engaged in nonphysical playground disputes solve their problems, leading them through steps that result in a peaceful solution. Solving interpersonal problems independent of adults is a responsible role. According to Judith M. Ferrara (1996), "A conflict resolution curriculum is aimed at improving student problem-solving skills, and will give students experience in practicing their skills and strategies" (19).

In the spring we ask all third graders interested in being a peer mediator to fill out an application. Its primary purpose is to obtain the names of the stu-

Figure 3–2. Scott leads the literature discussion group

dents who are interested, along with the parent's signature needed for permission to include the student. Completing the form helps the student feel that the job is important. We accept and train every applicant, since we are an inclusive organization.

In May, after sending out letters informing parents of the training schedule, we meet with new recruits for four hours over a two-week period. During the training program we teach the peer mediators how to carry out the negotiation process using ten steps:

1. Disputants agree to meet with mediators.
2. Disputants take a deep breath and calm down.
3. Mediators make introductions.
4. Mediators explain rules:
   a. Show respect.
   b. Don't interrupt each other.
5. Disputants tell what happened.
6. Mediators help disputants express how they feel using "I" messages (I feel that . . .).
7. Disputants brainstorm solutions.
8. Disputants choose a solution: mediators write it down.
9. Everyone shakes hands.
10. Mediators do follow-up next day/check in on parties involved.

We use role playing to help peer mediators become skillful negotiators. We demonstrate the techniques and show videos of previous peer mediators in action. In the fall, we review the ten mediation steps before kicking off the program.

I'm always looking for new ways to give students more responsibility. Julie told me she does not take attendance. One of her classroom jobs is Scanner. A student, not the teacher, fills in the computerized attendance sheet. I had never thought of that. After thirty-six years of recording attendance, I have handed that job over to a student. I'm always learning.

Encouraging Self-Discipline

One of my goals is to have every student act responsibly when I'm not in the classroom. If I'm needed to keep order, then students are under my control, not their own. I do not agonize over the one or two students who have difficulty with self-control; I never achieve one hundred percent. I simply rejoice that by January, most of the class, most of the time, exhibits self-discipline. How do I do it? I build a community (described in Chapter 2). I hand over responsibilities. I share control and have high expectations that students will practice self-control. I trust them and encourage them.

These approaches to self-discipline will not work unless the curriculum is engaging. When students are immersed in what they are doing, when they care about what they are doing, they forget about making mischief. They remain "on task," as we educators say. In this context, when students talk to each other and move about the room, the noise they make is the noise of learning.

What do I do with the student who doesn't exercise self-restraint? Sometimes I remove that student from the group. It does not solve the problem, but at least it enables the rest of the group to function. I have an obligation to provide an environment conducive to learning, and I will not allow a disruptive student to spoil it for everyone else.

When I'm feeling more tolerant, I try giving disruptive students leadership opportunities, and often they rise to the occasion. Rob was a child with low self-esteem, which he exhibited by bragging, clowning, and having to have the last word on every subject. At the same time, he was dramatic and had a talent for writing poetry. Rob volunteered for the job of poet-of-the-week and gave daily readings of poems he had written or discovered. The students and I applauded his performances. Even when he wasn't the poet-of-the-week, he was asked to share poems. I sent him to other classes as a model of how to read poetry with the correct pacing and expression. He became our expert poet-in-residence. It helped him overcome his need to tell us how great he was, because he felt like a valued member of the group. Because others were praising him, he did not need to disrupt the class with attention-seeking comments. Rob began to develop self-control out of a desire to be a member of the community. Every student has particular talents, and I try to draw on those talents to make the student feel important.

Allowing for Mistakes

In a caring classroom, it's okay to make mistakes. I concur with Alfie Kohn (1993), who says, "Mistakes offer information about how a student thinks. Correcting them quickly and efficiently doesn't do much to facilitate the learning process. More important, students who are afraid of making mistakes are unlikely to ask for help when they need it, unlikely to feel safe enough to take intellectual risks, and unlikely to be intrinsically motivated" (213). I want students to feel free to express their ideas even when others don't agree with them. They grow when they don't have to worry about being wrong. By expressing their opinions students gain self-confidence; they focus on learning rather than on the social dynamics of the classroom.

I want my students to realize that we all overlook things, misstep, and make mistakes. I actually encourage them to call my attention to those I make. Maggie reminded me that I did not have to pass out a new "Writers Record" sheet because we hadn't used both sides of the one we already had. "Thank you for pointing that out to me. What would I do without you?" Another time I was reading a novel aloud and misread a word. Betsy corrected me. I said, "Thank you, Betsy. I'm so glad you are following along so closely in your book." I am happy my students feel comfortable enough to correct my errors, and gently, as I do with them.

Because Julie Beers and I enjoy a secure, honest relationship, we can disagree amicably. For example, after I attended Karen Ernst's presentation at the 1997 IRA convention, I returned convinced of the value of connecting the visual arts to student's literacy development (described in detail in Chapter 9). Julie and I purchased sets of sketch books for our classes. To encourage our students to use the sketch pads, we gave a homework assignment: to draw a scene from C. S. Lewis' *The Lion, the Witch, and the Wardrobe*, which we were reading aloud to our classes. When Julie saw that many of her students had sketched drawings similar to those of the illustrator, she criticized them. "You can't copy. You have to do your own." I told Julie I thought it was a mistake to tell students not to look at the pictures in the book when sketching. I reminded her that art students learn to draw by going to the art museum and copying masterpieces. "Besides," I smiled, "I looked at the book to sketch my scene. I can't draw anything without looking at a picture."

Julie went back to her students, explained her discussion with me, and revised her earlier judgment. By making herself vulnerable and admitting she was in error, she strengthened her position in her classroom. She sends the message that learning involves trying out ideas and approaches. Making mistakes is part of the process.

Promoting Organizational Skills

By learning how to organize themselves, students become more independent and more likely to be successful. Forgetting homework, losing papers, running out of time drain children's creative energy.

At two long tables in our classroom, I've installed plastic file crates purchased at a local office supply store. I assign one crate to every four students, and give each student a set of hanging file folders labeled Social Science, Math, Health, Spelling, and Misc. These crates serve as "holding bins" for students' completed papers, long-term packets in mapping, and any other materials that need to be stored. (Papers needing corrections are attached to their clipboards

Figure 3–3. Mary files her papers in her crate

until students make the necessary changes, then filed.) Storing papers this way prevents the loss of items for student portfolios. The system works well, with just an occasional oral or written reminder (see Figure 3–3).

Linda Cooper, a fourth-grade colleague, gives her students a three-ring binder for organizing their papers. She divides binders into sections: Writing, Reading Record, Responses to Literature, Math, Science, Health, and Social Studies. This system eliminates crates and spiral notebooks because all the math papers, drafts of writing, mapping lessons, and other academic papers go into the notebooks. Linda is enthusiastic about this system. "This will be their student-led conference. Parents will see it all here, and it will eliminate a lot of sorting. Kids love it." Then she jokes, "The only drawback is that it took one hour to learn how to open and close the binders!"

When I first thought about this chapter, I titled it "Classroom Management." But soon I realized that I don't want to be a manager; I want to be the facilitator of an environment that encourages responsible learners. I want to reduce students' reliance on me. Fostering independence and building a community go together. "You can't have one without the other."

4

Writing Our Stories

In the fall, a visiting teacher asked my students, "What is your secret to success in writing? What makes you good writers?"

MAGGIE: We've been writing since kindergarten.
JESSIE: We write every day.
BAKARI: We get to choose our own topics.
MOLLIE: It's fun! I like to share what I write.
HANNAH: We know how to use a thesaurus to get interesting vocabulary.
JOHN: We teach our kindergarten pals how to write by asking them questions and helping them spell big words.
ELI: We give suggestions to each other to make our writing better.

The students' answers express my beliefs about what I need to provide as their writing teacher. In the fall, students come to fourth grade with varied experience in writing. Some students have been crafting pieces on self-selected topics since kindergarten; others have been assigned traditional research and book reports and have little or no experience with revising and editing. Some have been writing almost daily, others much less frequently. The background and ability range widely. In the past, such a potpourri of needs would have been reason for dismay. Now I am excited about being a teacher who can make a difference. In *A Fresh Look at Writing*, Donald Graves (1994) says that "if students had one good teacher of writing in their entire career, irrespective of grade level, they could be successful writers" (14).

I have read many of the professional books and articles by Donald Graves, Lucy Calkins, Nancie Atwell, Ralph Fletcher, Georgia Heard, and others. In attempting to implement their ideas, often failing, I have gained enough experience to fill a dozen books. By attending professional conferences and talking with my colleagues, I have revised what I believe and practice. I have arrived at a set of beliefs about how to foster proficient writers:

- Sharing a rich array of literature provides models for writers.
- Guiding class discussions about what writers do encourages good writing.
- Providing authentic purposes for writing motivates students.
- Revealing myself as a writer demonstrates that writing is a lifelong pursuit.
- Writing every day is an important aspect of becoming proficient.
- Including minilessons on particular problems or skills demonstrates the mechanics and craft of writing.
- Providing tools, such as thesauruses, spell checkers, Alpha-Smarts, computers, dictionaries, sample formats, and a variety of writing materials assists students in the process.
- Offering students choices—in topics, audience, and genres—encourages enthusiasm.
- Peer conferencing provides valuable suggestions.
- Revising and editing allows students to take responsibility for their pieces.
- Gathering together to share and celebrate writing builds communities.

In a classroom that incorporates these beliefs, students fall in love with writing. Writing class becomes their favorite part of the day. When students care about what they are doing, they want to do it. They want to learn how to make their readers care.

In 1996, when Regie Routman gave me a spiral notebook and told me to write down my observations, thoughts, and reflections to "free the writer within," she had never read anything I had written. She only knew I had things to say. She believed I could write. I need to convey that same affirmation to my students. Because they have things to say that others will want to hear, they need to write. I believe they are all capable of writing powerfully. I am reminded of Elena's description of her adoption.

Dear Mom,

Do you remember the day I came home?
　Well, I will tell you again.
　"Here she comes!" people exclaimed.
　Off the plane walked a brown-haired beauty.
　You were crying, not because you were sad, but because you were happy.
　You were so happy to be a mom. It was the day you had been waiting for. It was finally here.

Tears streaming down your cheeks.
So proud of yourself for becoming a mother.
I feel lucky to have a mom like you.
You with your beautiful blue eyes that sparkle in the light.
Your spectacular smile that stretched across your face.
I love you.

Love,
Elena

Elena gave this tribute to her mother for Mother's Day.

Creating a Climate for Writing

"How do I get started? What do I do first?" These are the questions most frequently asked by teachers observing my writing class. But long before I ever get to procedures, I try to create a climate that encourages writing.

Sharing Models of Good Writing

I begin by reading and reading and reading to kids, helping them realize that they too have wonderful things to say. We have lots of conversations about poetry books, picture books, and fiction. We talk about the way language is used. I say things like,

- Listen to the lead.
- Didn't that grab your attention?
- I love this sentence.
- Listen again to that description.
- Oh, that's the perfect word.
- What a writer. Awesome!

We talk about the power of language to touch our deepest feelings. I usually read them *Love You Forever* by Robert Munsch, a simple picture book I can never get through without crying. I tell my students about my son, Mark. When he read this book aloud to a church congregation on Mother's Day, there were audible sobs in the audience.

Then I read aloud *Always Wear Clean Underwear!* by Marc Gillman, a hilarious book that is perfect for fourth graders. We all laugh together.

I search for books the class can connect with and vary my selections according to the students' reactions. As Frank Smith remarks in *Joining the Literacy Club*, books are models of good writing that enable students to learn from authors. Here are some favorites to begin the year:

- *When I Was Your Age: Original Stories About Growing Up*, edited by Amy Ehrlich. Humorous and poignant short stories about the childhoods of famous children's authors.
- *Purr . . . Children's Book Illustrators Brag About Their Cats*, edited by Michael J. Rosen. Forty-three artists celebrate their most memorable felines with illustrations and dialogue.
- *Owen* by Kevin Henkes. Picture book about mouse parents who try to get their son to give up his favorite blanket before he starts school.
- *Lives of the Writers: Comedies, Tragedies (and What the Neighbors Thought)* by Kathleen Krull. The inside scoop on twenty famous writers written with wit and style.
- *Who Was That Masked Man, Anyway?* by Avi. A funny book written entirely in dialogue and perfect to read aloud.

Once we have read some good books together, we launch our writing class.

Discussing What Writers Do

Because I build lessons on what my students already know when they arrive in my classroom, I begin each year by talking about good writers and what they do. One class came up with this impressive list, a testament to good teaching in earlier grades:

Good writers:
- make their story interesting
- make mistakes
- describe what is happening so well the reader believes it is true
- make the story come alive
- hold the reader's interest
- have well-developed characters
- take their time writing a piece
- reread/revise [my contribution]
- share their ideas
- make a catchy title
- ask for suggestions
- get ideas from books

I copy this list onto chart paper so we can add to it as the year progresses. We discuss each additional point and examples from books and student writing. By the end of the school year, the list reflects what students have learned from minilessons, discussions, and being writers themselves. Some June additions were:

- uses descriptive vocabulary
- uses catchy leads
- uses thesaurus
- edits
- has closure
- uses details
- writes about what she/he knows
- uses point of view
- writes with voice (personality)
- uses dialogue well
- can write in several genres
- uses sentence variety

All year we talk about good writing, whether for five minutes or twenty. I bring in any newspaper articles on writers I find, most recently one about R. L. Stine, the author of the Goosebump series, who says he cranks out books so frequently because he sits down and writes twenty pages every morning. This led to a discussion about how often and how much writers write, which broadened further to include the question of quality in popular series. I don't plan these discussions. I simply take advantage of every opportunity.

Finding Authentic Purposes for Writing

Students need authentic reasons for writing. Occasionally I assign a topic, but it is vital that students also consider it important.

When asked to write letters of recommendation for Michele Raeder, our student teacher, to put in her portfolio, students revised with passion. They wanted to help her get her first teaching job (see Figure 4–1).

When Jessica did an interview for the school newspaper, a publication read schoolwide, she worked hard.

A, B, C, D, E, F, G—HAVE YOU MET MS. FERZETTI?

By Jessica Herzfeld

With a warm smile, Ms. Ferzetti welcomes me to her Kindergarten classroom and seats me at her desk.

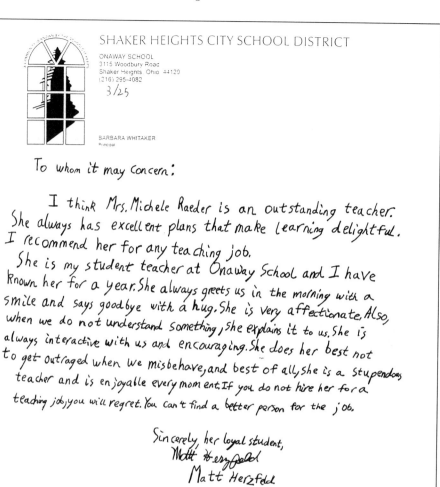

SHAKER HEIGHTS CITY SCHOOL DISTRICT

ONAWAY SCHOOL
3115 Woodbury Road
Shaker Heights, Ohio 44120
(216) 295-4082

3/25

BARBARA WHITAKER
Principal

To whom it may concern:

I think Mrs. Michele Raeder is an outstanding teacher. She always has excellent plans that make learning delightful. I recommend her for any teaching job.
She is my student teacher at Onaway School and I have known her for a year. She always greets us in the morning with a smile and says goodbye with a hug. She is very affectionate. Also, when we do not understand something, she explains it to us. She is always interactive with us and encouraging. She does her best not to get outraged when we misbehave, and best of all, she is a stupendous teacher and is enjoyable every moment. If you do not hire her for a teaching job, you will regret. You can't find a better person for the job.

Sincerely, her loyal student,
Matt Herzfeld
Matt Herzfeld

Figure 4–1. Letter of recommendation for student teacher

Ms. Ferzetti grew up in Southampton, Pennsylvania with two older brothers, one sister, her parents and a cat. When she was young, she would romp and frolic in the woods. Her childhood is a wonderful memory, and one she will cherish forever.

The years went by, and soon Ms. Ferzetti had her masters in elementary education.

But Ms. Ferzetti still keeps in touch with her childhood friends and all the friends she's made since. She calmly told me she had written 45 friendly letters over the past weekend.

Reading and writing go hand in hand. If you're a good reader, most likely you're a good writer too, or the other way around. Ms. Ferzetti enjoys both reading and writing and is great at doing both.

She thinks she is a good friend because she keeps in touch with her friends and is a good listener. As I look at the smiling faces of the happy kindergartners, I know she is a good friend and a wonderful person.

Sometimes students select a genre I haven't even thought about. Inspired by Julie's class, my students decided to produce a monthly newsletter for parents based on "Time for Kids," a weekly student newsletter. The students voted on a name, "Classroom Update," and decided upon the following elements once they had examined the "Time for Kids" format.

- Did You Know?
- Quote of the Month
- Jokes and Riddles
- Cartoons (done by Nick, our cartoonist)
- Crossword Puzzle
- List of Good Books
- Short Stories
- Trivia Box
- Interview
- People Talk Back (encouraging parents and other readers to write back)
- Mystery Person
- Teacher Talk (letter from me—I asked for this)

As they continued to read "Time for Kids" and articles from our local newspaper, the students took notes. These were their observations:

- a picture is helpful
- written in columns
- paragraphs are indented
- heading on articles
- pictures have captions or labels
- articles are typed
- some pictures are drawings
- headings give clues to content of article
- graphs are included
- sub headings sometimes
- some facts in a box (for Did You Know?)
- interesting first sentences catch your attention
- most articles are short

- mostly articles have facts and information
- interesting topics
- quotes are throughout

I also taught a minilesson about good journalism using examples and asking students what the writers did. Our list:

- catchy headlines
- leads that capture reader's interest
- who, what, where, when, why
- closing statement
- descriptive vocabulary
- sometimes humor

Students referred to the list during conferences when they were making suggestions for improvement and at the end of writing class when we shared examples of catchy headlines, humor, and other elements of good journalism from their class work.

Students volunteered to write the articles, and some paired up on articles, jokes, and tabulating survey results. My role, in addition to encouraging well-written articles by sharing models, was to do the final editing on the computer and to paste the articles on the master layout for duplication. Copies went to parents, administrators, teachers, and to Julie's class.

Colleen Brady, a parent, sent a postcard to the class.

What a terrific newsletter! As a working mom I sometimes can't keep up with all the school news and local news. I now have a NEW source—the Classroom Update. I enjoyed the articles and artwork. I must admit my favorite article was the Natural History Museum's animals—I wonder why? [Her daughter wrote that article.]

We produced the newsletter each month throughout the year, and although it was time-consuming, the interest level was high. Some issues had a theme, such as "Traditions" in December. Collaborating with Julie's class was helpful because it gave the students ideas for improvement. Next year if the class is interested, we will do it again but maybe every other month in order to give us more time for other kinds of writing:

- letters of sympathy
- letters to pen pals
- letters to cities in Ohio for information to use in the study of Ohio
- thank-you cards
- interviews published in school newspaper

- book reviews to be put on a bulletin board in hall recommending books to other students
- report writing to be presented orally to another class
- poem for Father's Day gift
- "Moment with Mother" to be given as Mother's Day gift
- a short piece of writing to be used as a benchmark for parent conference
- poems and stories to be published in anthology or magazines that publish student writing
- letters of recommendation for student teacher
- poems for an assembly
- Reader's Theater to be performed for school
- business letters for information about prairie states we're studying
- speeches to be given in class for students and parents
- stories of interest to the student
- biographies for display and highlights shared orally
- invitations

Students don't care about everything they write. Sometimes I see a student sitting and staring at a piece of blank paper. I talk to the student. If it is a case of writer's block I might say "What do you care a lot about?" or "What do you spend lots of time doing?" Usually my help and a good model piece is all the student needs. But sometimes I am not successful. I will ask the student to complete the written piece if it is an assignment, such as a benchmark piece for portfolios.

Revealing Myself as a Writer

When I join my students to write, I am able to speak about writing with an authentic voice. I show them my rough drafts of this book, of letters I have written to parents. I tell them I don't like to revise but I do it because I want to write something people will understand and enjoy. When students compare my revisions and my earlier draft, they see improvement.

Apparently I have been successful in getting this point across, because Justin asked, "Mrs. Servis, you tell us it is taking you over a year to write your book because you revise so much. What I want to know is why R. L. Stine can publish a book every month?"

My response was, "Good question, Justin. When you are as famous as R. L. Stine you can pay people to help you revise. I'm sure his first book took much longer to write than a month. Why don't you write to him and ask him?"

During writing workshop, when I can grab some time, I write alongside my students. Sometimes I ask them to give me a few minutes because I'm writing my pen pal or I'm writing an article for the newsletter. Because I write every day, I can tell them

- I wrote a letter to Daniel last night. I told him a package is in the mail.
- Listen to my lead on my story about horseback riding. Does it grab your attention?
- I brought in my rough draft for the letter I'm writing to parents. See how much revision I did?

I share what I have learned as a writer and encourage my students to do likewise.

Writing Daily

In *A Fresh Look at Writing*, Donald Graves comments that

> If students are not engaged in writing at least four days out of five, and for a period of thirty-five to forty minutes, beginning in first grade, they will have little opportunity to learn to think through the medium of writing. (1994, 104)

I know how important daily writing is. If I miss more than a day, I lose momentum. Graves goes on to say that students "need daily writing time to be able to move their pieces along until they accomplish what they set out to do" (105).

Because scheduling constraints and interruptions often cut into our writing time, I sometimes bring writing into other parts of the day. I may combine it with literature, spelling, or content areas to ensure a block of time (boldface print denotes these times). Here is a typical schedule:

9:05	Morning Routine (copying a daily "Things to Do" list from the overhead, turning in homework)
9:15	PA Announcements/Attendance
9:20	**Math**
10:10	SS (social studies, science, health)
11:15	Read Aloud
11:30	Specials (music, physical education, art, library)
12:15	Lunch
1:05	DIRT (Daily Individual Reading Time)
1:30	Poetry (poet-of-the-week reads poetry aloud)
1:35	Writing Class
2:20	**Reading** (Guided) Tuesday, Thursday
	Spelling Monday, Wednesday
	Reading with Pals Friday
3:10	Read Aloud/Closure for the day
3:25	Home

Setting Up and Managing a Writing Class

Certain routines aid students in becoming proficient writers. My daily routine for writing period goes this way:

minilesson: when I teach a procedure or a lesson on the craft of writing to the whole class (approximately five to ten minutes)

writing: when students are drafting, conferring, revising, editing individually or in pairs (thirty minutes)

sharing: when we come together as a group for a wrap-up (ten minutes)

All three parts add to the students' growth in writing. Minilessons provide knowledge. Writing time lets students put thoughts down, reflect, and rethink. Group feedback provides encouragement to continue.

Providing the Tools of Writers

The following list is a sample of some of the resources I find helpful in a writing class:

- Writing Notebook: a three-ring binder with dividers and notebook paper. The sections includes forms, minilessons, ideas for topics, letters, poetry, fiction, nonfiction, misc. Students include all rough drafts, revised drafts, and copies of the published pieces. The outside is decorated with the student's pictures and personal memorabilia.
- Alpha-Smarts: small, inexpensive writing processors used by students to type final copy that are then transferred electronically through a cord connected to the computer for printout. Our classroom set is an asset in the production of our monthly newsletter.
- Spell checker: handheld electronic "dictionary," but quicker and easier for students to use.
- Dictionaries: *Scholastic Rhyming Dictionaries* and traditional dictionaries students use when the handheld spell checkers are not available.
- Thesauruses: a resource for alternative nouns and verbs to replace "over-worked" vocabulary.
- Paper: lined and unlined for a multitude of uses, stationery for friendly letters, school stationery for business letters.
- Pens: fine-tipped colored felt pens for editing, highlighters for emphasizing text during minilessons, black pens for final version when a student desires to hand copy a piece rather than use an Alpha-Smart.
- Computer: for word processing.
- Formats: models of business letters, friendly letters, book reviews, letter of recommendation, and others (see Figure 4–2).

BOOK REVIEW FORMAT

Headline:

Title, author, illustrator, publisher, number of pages, price, ages, (child's book)

Catchy lead
Describe main characters / or main character
Tell the problem (if fiction)
Type of book:
     (biogaphy, mystery, fantasy, fairy tales, folktales, picture book)
May include illustration from book
Opinion
If recommend or not
Closing

Name of reviewer: (why they know or have fame to warrant an opinion)
Example: author of certain book
               critic
               expert in some area

Figure 4–2. Book Review Format

- Books:
  1. For giving students reasons to write letters:
     Freebies for Kids: Something for Nothing or Next to Nothing, by the editors of *Freebies* magazine
     Free Stuff for Kids: Hundreds of Free and Up-to-a-Dollar Things Kids Can Send for by Mail!, by Free Stuff editors
     How to Reach Your Favorite Sports Star, by Larry Strauss
     The Kids Address Book: Over 3,000 Addresses of Celebrities, Athletes, Entertainers, and More . . . Just for Kids!, by Michael Levine

2. For giving students unusual formats to use as models for writing books:

   If, by Sarah Perry. If cats could fly, if hummingbirds told secrets, if spiders could read braille, and other delightful thoughts with illustrations.

   Fun No Fun, by James Stevenson. An autobiographical picture book.

   The Kids' Business Book, by Arlene Erlbach. Ideas about how to start your own business.

   Totally Fun Things to Do with Your Dog, by Maxine Rock. Training tips and activities.

   Wildlife Rescue: The Work of Dr. Kathleen Ramsay, by Jennifer Owings Dewey. A photo essay.

3. For giving students ideas for their own poems:

   Mississippi Mud, by Ann Turner. Prairie poems

   All the Small Poems and Fourteen More, by Valerie Worth. Poems about everyday items

   Joyful Noise, by Paul Fleischman. Nature poems

   On the Wing, by Douglas Florian. Bird poems

All year I go to bookstores and libraries looking for books that will inspire students to write, and I urge students to do the same.

Conducting Minilessons

I design minilessons to clarify a genre we're studying or to focus on a strategy students need to know or use better. Some of my minilessons:

- capturing a moment: short descriptive memorable moment
- using the senses to describe a situation or setting: sight, sound, taste, smell, touch
- using dialogue effectively
- writing good leads
- writing good endings
- avoiding overworked words: how do we find others?
- finding a good title
- using voice in our writing
- working for sentence variety
- writing a friendly letter
- writing a business letter

During the minilesson students take notes in their writer's notebook, so they can refer back to them later. A student might also teach a minilesson. For example, a former student taught the class how to edit using the overhead and a transparency of his written piece.

In the beginning of the school year, my minilessons demonstrate procedures and writing rules. The class and I talk about what rules we need and why, and make a list together. When I suggest a rule, I make sure students understand my rationale and have a chance to comment. For example, I ask the students to write on every other line on one side of the paper only and to use double space on the computer. Why? It makes revising and editing easier. I show my own rough drafts as models. Here are some others:

- Save everything, all rough drafts edited and revised, and put them in your writing notebook.
- Date and label everything.
- Document every piece of writing on your writing record (see Figure 4–3).
- Do your best in spelling and punctuation as you write.
- Always reread what you have written.
- Whisper during writing class because we need quiet when we write.
- Self-edit in a color different from the print of your text. (I senior edit in another color.)
- Fill out a daily writing record listing what you have accomplished (see Figure 4–4).

Although I look to Donald Graves, Nancie Atwell, and others for minilesson ideas, the students often don't apply these lessons until they have a "need to know." When I cover fiction writing, a favorite with students, they need to know about dialogue, so in a minilesson I teach the whole class how to write it. Sometimes an individual student needs to learn a strategy, which usually comes to my attention during conferences. I teach the student immediately, one-on-one.

Offering Choices

Through experience I have discovered that students have their own ideas on what they'd like to write about and like making their own choices. I only need to give them permission and some inspiration.

At the beginning of October I talked about the writing I had done in September, including

- notes to Ray Coutu, my editor at Heinemann
- a sympathy card with note to Mrs. Jindra, a teacher in our building
- postcards to my grandsons
- rubrics to use for assessment (I showed them some)
- my book drafts (which I share regularly)
- thank-you notes
- a story about my bad experience on a horse

W R I T I N G R E C O R D

Title/Topic	Audience	Genre	Date Started	Date Ended	What Happened to the piece?
School supply poem	Class / Parents	poetry	8/28	9/2	Bulletin Bd
Camp Stories	Class	Fiction	9/12	9/24	—
Alpine Tundra	Class	report	9/23	10/3	Bulletin Bd.
Classroom Update	Parents	news articles	10/20	10/30	Newsletter
Plant Research	Class	script	10/10	10/30	Presentation
Pen Pal letter	Pen Pal	friendly letter	10/7		mailed it
Raisin Bran	Cereal Company	Business letter	10/12		mailed it
S60RR	High School	Poetry	10/23	10/30	magazine
Classroom Update	Parents	Short story	11/3	12/9	newsletter
Goals	Teacher Parents	Goals	11/13	11/17	report card
Business /Ohio	Class	Business letter	1/5	1/6	mailed it
Business /Ohio	Class	Business letter	1/12	1/12	mailed it
Classroom Update	Parents	news articles	1/26	1/29	newsletter
Pen Pal letter	Pen Pal	friendly letter	1/29		mailed it
January	Class	poem	1/16	1/29	read aloud
Kangaroos	teacher	report	12/5	12/6	turned in
Cats	Pals	Fiction	12/10	2/8	book
Martin Luther King Jr.	School Assembly	Play Biography	1/5	1/20	Performed
Reading /Sarah Plain & Tall	Class	Readers theater	1/7	1/18	Performed

Figure 4–3. Writing Record Documentation

WRITING RECORD
What did I work on today?

Name: *Laura* _____

Week of _5/20_____	Week of _5/28_____
Monday Today I started writing my final copy narrative and shared my writing narrative to Ms. Beers' Class	**Monday** MEMORIAL DAY
Tuesday Today I copy writing finished my final narrative started my math narrative, and I peer confereneed.	**Tuesday** Today I worked on my math narrative and brainstormed for S.S.
Wednesday Today I shared my reading narrative to Ms. Nagy's class and finished my math narrative rough draft.	**Wednesday** Today I worked on editing and re-editing my math narrative
Thursday Today I edited my math narrative.	**Thursday** Today I peer conferenc and worked on writing my math narrative final copy.
Friday Dr. Weltman is sharing her rough drafts and revisions for her P.H.D. thesis	**Friday** Today I finished writing my math narrative and started SS/Heath rough draft.

Figure 4–4. Writing Record

- success cards, the affirmation cards I mail to parents
- letters to family and friends
- grocery list for husband
- weekly menu of meals I prepare
- list of responsibilities for student teacher

These details help students see that topics are all around them in everyday events. As Don Graves (1994) emphasizes, "Writing comes from the events of our daily lives, from what appears at first glance to be trivial" (36). Last fall, Glenn, a student in Julie Beers' class, suggested that everyone write a letter to Onaway's former principal, Rosemary Weltman. The students missed her special hugs and attention and leaped at the opportunity to let her know. A sample letter:

> Dear Dr. Weltman,
>
> I regret not seeing you as much as I had hoped. This morning I was very excited when Glenn brought up writing to you.
>
> Do you remember my rat Lou? Well, she got cancer so we had to put her to sleep. I got a new one named Munchkin (a.k.a. Munchy) but a week and three days after I got him he choked and died. I got a new rat named Miss Mocha Fudge. I thought you might want to know.
>
> Do you like your new job? I hope you do. I haven't got to meet the new principal very much.
>
> Hope I see you soon,
> Madeline Weinland

Dr. Weltman wrote Madeline back. "I was so sad to read about Lou and Munchy. I am hoping that Miss Mocha Fudge (great name!) maintains better health!" Most fourth graders enjoy getting mail and like writing letters if they get a response.

Students keep an ongoing list of topic ideas in their writing notebooks. They decorate the front and back covers with special pictures and memorabilia, which also spark ideas for stories. By reminding students to revisit their lists of possible topics and by sharing books, I hope that most students will have more topics than time. Many carry their writing notebooks home to work on pieces.

Too often we limit students by assigning topics, maintaining that this will produce better writing. But if I want my students to be as passionate about what they write as I am, I must allow them to decide for themselves.

Peer Conferences

Because I don't have time to confer with every student every day, I teach students how to help each other. With a student volunteer I model a peer conference. The class watches, paying particular attention to what I say to the writer about her draft. The student reads her piece aloud and then I make suggestions: perhaps she needs to think of a stronger lead or to add more description. I remind students that my notes on good journalism or fiction help me frame my suggestions.

Students can have a one-to-one conference when they need one—they don't have to wait until they finish—but I ask them to sit apart from classmates who are composing, since their talk is distracting. If I'm available, I will listen and make suggestions. As the year progresses the students get better at listening and making suggestions.

Revising and Editing

At the beginning of each writing class, students reread their previous day's writing. I always tell them how amazed I am when I return to what I thought was excellent writing on the previous day only to find that it has problems. I stress the importance of revision but make it clear that the revisions are entirely up to the student. I tell them, "You are the author." When students care about their writing, they willingly revise again and again. So often it depends on whether they could decide on their own topic.

Students start the year a bit confused about the difference between revision and editing. Revision focuses on changing the content, expanding a section, adding or deleting details, and finding effective interesting vocabulary.

In my experience, students resist revision. They don't always see where their writing is unclear or realize that readers have only the words on the page to tell them what the writer wants them to know. It's a gradual process, and most students will never revise as much as the teacher thinks they should.

Editing, in contrast, is correcting spelling, punctuation, capitalization, and paragraphing. Like Nancie Atwell, I require students to edit with a colored pen and to use the common editing symbols. When a student believes she has made all corrections, she puts the writing in a designated basket. Later, in what I call senior editing, I look for errors, using a different colored pen. I usually sit with the student. To help with the volume, I use parent volunteers. If I feel that a student did not spend enough time editing, I ask her to go over her writing again. I expect appropriate diligence in editing.

Not every written piece goes through senior editing. Pen pal letters are written and mailed out promptly, with errors or not. Pieces written for oral presentation, such as speeches, don't require editing.

Sharing and Celebrating

During the last few minutes of writing class I ask students to return to their tables for our sharing time. All attention is on the student who volunteers to read his writing. I never require a student to read aloud. This is the time we share revisions, recognizing how students improved the flow of sentences, developed stronger conclusions, or tried out especially vivid words. This encourages others. I want my students to see and hear how revising makes writing better. I tell them what Nancie Atwell (1998) says: "Crossing out is tough—it still kills me to admit a chunk of my text needs to go—but writers need to be tough-minded if they're to get better at writing" (163).

When Tessa was writing a piece about her dog, she asked the class for help in revision. The sentences she read aloud were

"Arrr," yelped my dog at a large fear of the high wooden playground. She stepped back noticing no way to get down from the ledge.

The students told Tessa she needed descriptive details because they didn't get a clear picture of the dog or of the situation. With help from students, Tessa revised her sentences to read

"Arr," yelped my dog, a medium-sized yellow lab, fearing the high splintered wooden playground. She perked up her ears, stepped back frightened, noticing no way to get down from the lofty ledge.

These final moments are also a time of celebration. I ask students to share things I have noticed about their writing in our conferences, such as a particularly descriptive paragraph, a catchy lead, the rhythm created by varying sentences, and other examples of powerful writing. I invite reluctant students to share a small part of their writing. We all applaud good writing because we know the amount of effort behind it.

What About Spelling?

Our society values correct spelling. Poor spelling is a roadblock to meaning. It obscures and confuses what we're trying to say. If students misspell words in their writing, parents, thinking of the future, become anxious. I try to maintain high expectations when it comes to spelling.

Spelling and editing go together. Students spend a large portion of their time correcting misspelled words using the dictionary or a handheld spell checker. I ask them to circle all the words they think are spelled incorrectly and check the spelling. They write the correct spelling over the circled word with a colored pen. Most students can recognize which words aren't spelled correctly. Every year, however, I have at least one student who finds spelling difficult, cannot recognize which words are misspelled, and writes pieces full of spelling errors. If I expect students like these to correct every misspelled word, not only will they not improve their spelling, but they will write short pieces to avoid such a laborious process. For these students I do more senior editing.

Because of the volume of writing we do and because I expect that written assignments in every subject will be free of spelling errors, as the year progresses the students become better spellers. Repeatedly seeing a word spelled correctly enables students to recognize a misspelling. My role, as a spelling teacher, is to help students recognize when a word is spelled incorrectly and to ask them to use a tool like a dictionary to correct it. This is how the adult world functions.

About four times a year, without warning, I give a "benchmark" spelling test. I read aloud two paragraphs from a fourth-grade level book (usually one of the reading books), and students write down the sentences as I dictate. I ask them to reread the paragraphs and circle all the words they would use a dictionary to check. I also tell them to check over the punctuation. Then I collect the papers. By examining these tests I can see if a student recognizes misspelled words and adds common punctuation. Over the year, I note progress. When I share these benchmark tests with parents, I stress that this reflects how their child spells on a regular basis and that it has more validity than being able to spell a list of memorized words. I point out that a list of random words remembered on Friday is forgotten by Monday. Parents agree.

Benchmarks and editing are not all I do in the area of spelling. Every week, usually on Monday, I teach a minilesson about a spelling rule that I notice students have problems with, such as *i before e except after c* and ask students at each table to brainstorm a list of words that follow the rule. (I refer to J. Richard Gentry's [1997] list of spelling rules in *My Kid Can't Spell!* Also, Faye Bolton and Diane Snowball's *Ideas for Spelling* [1993] and *Teaching Spelling* [1993] are helpful.) Students refer extensively to dictionaries in this exercise. Each table puts the list on the board. The rest of us point out any errors we see and then we all discuss the words. For homework that evening, students use some of the words in sentences.

Later in the week, I use these sentences for a dictation exercise. I choose five to read aloud. The students write them down, attempting to spell and punctuate correctly. Then they team up with an assigned partner to proofread and edit the dictation. When they agree that their sentences are perfect, they bring them to me. I look at the papers and give them a score according to the total errors on both. We call the exercise Golf, because we want the lowest score—zero errors. The students work hard to receive a zero. This game gives students further practice in editing and proofreading, and it also reinforces the rules of grammar because partners explain to each other why they have used certain punctuation. I often hear, "A comma belongs here because we're separating items on a list" or "We need quotation marks here because someone is talking."

Once a week I set aside thirty-five minutes for playing spelling games. Julie Beers and I have bought a number of games, such as Hangman (Milton Bradley), Boggle (Parker Brothers), Scrabble (Milton Bradley), Upwords (Milton Bradley), Pass the Bomb (Gibson's Games), and Spelling Bee (Creative Teaching Association), and share them between our two classrooms. If I try to skip this weekly routine, the students remind me—they enjoy it.

Every summer Julie and I spend hours reviewing and revising our spelling programs. We have concluded that

- Our students improve in spelling because they do a lot of writing in our classes.
- Examining words carefully helps students recognize common spelling patterns, suffixes, prefixes, and compound words.
- It is important to expect correct spelling in all written assignments.
- We want students to develop a lifelong habit of referring to dictionaries and spell checkers.
- We expect students to memorize frequently used words (we use the high utility five-hundred word list put together by Rebecca Sitton [1998]).

Faye Bolton and Diane Snowball (1993) summarize our viewpoint well: "Accuracy in spelling is a gradual process that is acquired through trial and error, modeling by adults and peers, hypothesis testing and opportunities for practice" (21).

Assessing Writing

Every day, students assess their writing by rereading what they wrote the previous day and revising. They give each other suggestions for improvement, and I work with them in conferences. We talk about good writing and we listen to examples of good writing. Students are knowledgeable about what writers need to do. Through daily writing they make progress. Assessment is ongoing.

My school district requires letter grades in writing. It seems impossible to assign fair grades, since all students are making steady progress and I am unwilling to discourage anyone, so I asked the other fourth-grade teachers to help me create a rubric for assessing writing. The rubric would provide us with a standard, by listing criteria in the form of indicators.

In the fall I used minilessons to teach and demonstrate each indicator. For example, students need to know exactly what it means when teachers say, "Your piece needs more details." What constitutes a detail? Terms like these need to be defined and illustrated especially when students and teachers used the rubric to

Assessment Rubric for 4th grade Writing			
indicators	consistent	inconsistent	comments
Sticks to topic	✓		letter to Post company
Has logical development & makes sense	✓		Wow article / Jitters of PP tot
Uses descriptive vocabulary	✓		Jitters of PP test / Wow article
Includes details	✓		Jitters of PP test
Uses correct format		✓	newsletter / business letter Correct
Contains a creative lead	✓		Math made yummy
Includes a strong ending	✓		letter to Post company
Proofreads a rough draft and edits	✓		Math made yummy
Takes responsibility for revising	✓		Jitters article of PP test
Mechanics		✓	
Spells almost all words correctly	✓		Jitters of PP test
Uses capital letters correctly	✓		Math made yummy
Uses correct punctuation		✓	
Shows an emerging awareness of paragraphing by grouping like ideas	✓		fashion book page 2

Figure 4–5. Writing Rubric

evaluate progress. Each trimester, students review the writing pieces in their notebooks to identify examples of their growth (see Figure 4–5).

If a student can provide evidence that he or she meets all the indicators, this translates into an A. (Each indicator is worth approximately 10 percent.) If I disagree with a student, we discuss our conflicting views and come to a joint decision. I respect my students' opinions. In fact, they often tend to be too hard on themselves, and I need to point out their strengths and encourage them. Jenny, a student who enjoyed writing poetry, overlooked the descriptive language in assessing her poem. I had to point this out to her.

My role is to encourage my students to be better writers and to help them see exactly what they are contributing to that process. Like Don Graves (1994), who put away his red pen, "I have also shifted from keeping all the records myself to helping children maintain records that will provide concrete evidence that they are becoming better writers" (169).

The temperature was 90 degrees: fans were blowing hot air around, the shades were drawn to keep out the sun, recess noise was coming through the open windows, and the students had been writing Onaway memories for our June newsletter for an hour and a half. Boys and girls were lying on the rug with pencils and paper, writing and revising. Students sat at desks editing, and pairs were in peer-conference huddles. Fingers were pressing the keys of the Alpha-Smarts as others typed final pieces. I called out, "It's time to clean up and gather on the rug."

All I heard were moans. Why, with only eight days left in the school year, had nobody asked to go out for recess? How can students sustain such hard work under difficult conditions? My conclusions are simple. The students care about what they are doing. They have stories to tell. I provide the environment that enables them to tell their stories. It can happen in every classroom.

5

Becoming Proficient Readers

The following article appeared in our classroom newspaper for March:

Book Club Bragging
by Mary Holmes

All right, so I won't brag, but the book club March 4 was a humongous success. It was held at 3005 Montgomery Rd. and half the class attended. We were discussing *All About Sam* by Lois Lowry. Lois Lowry has also written a series of books about Anastasia, Sam's big sister, so if you liked *All About Sam*, be sure to check them out.

We all got totally into the questions, especially the one, "Do you think when babies cry they are trying to communicate like Sam in the story?" Everyone was telling stories about their little brothers or sisters and when they were babies. "We only got to a few questions because they were questions that made us think," said Mollie Silver. "Oh, the food was good, too," she added.

After about half an hour, we took a short break for snacks. Then we got back to the questions. "I thought it was great," commented Jessie Schiller, who attended the book club. "It was a good discussion and it wasn't all girls. Last time it was almost all girls."

For the other half of the class that didn't make it, be sure to catch the next one! We hope the whole class comes next time.

I attended this event, but as an observer. Mary Holmes, the student leader, organized the entire evening. She gave out invitations to the class, found out who needed rides, and planned the questions and activities. What prompted fourth graders to discuss books outside of school time? Primarily their enthusiasm for reading. (Of course, the promise of snacks fuels that enthusiasm.) The students in Julie Beers' class had come up with the idea. In the fall, they invited two of our class members, Hannah and Matt, to attend their first book club. The two came back brimming with ideas for forming a club of our own. I encouraged them, and our first meeting to discuss Jane Leslie Conly's *Rasco and the Rats of NIMH* was held at Hannah's home in December. Are all my students enthusiastic, proficient readers who attend book clubs after hours? No, but I'm working on it!

What I Believe Is Important

When I was a child, reading for pleasure was something that happened at home. At school I read basal readers and textbooks. The basals were boring and the textbooks provided only facts, no feelings. Nonetheless, I began my teaching career using basals because I didn't know what else to use. Converting to literature has been a long-term process. What was missing in the days of basal readers was the joy, the rich vocabulary, and the emotional involvement that results from reading whole, high-quality books, rather than excerpts from books. My students are fortunate because good literature has a prominent place in our day. We are surrounded by books. We talk about books. Through reading we visit other worlds, learn about our own world, and even search for purpose in our lives.

By planning real literature at the heart of the curriculum, I provide an environment that encourages reading for pleasure. In addition, I

- allow my students to see me reading.
- talk about what I'm reading with my students.
- surround my students with books and magazines.
- provide time daily for self-selected reading in class.
- read aloud poems, picture books, and novels.
- talk about new additions to our classroom library and show them to the class.
- provide weekly time for peer conferences about books students have completed.
- listen to individuals tell me about a good book.
- use literature discussion groups to discuss assigned literature.
- assign thirty minutes of self-selected reading as daily homework.
- teach reading strategies to assist comprehension.
- talk about authors (their style, choice of genre, life, and interests).
- help students find books at their independent reading level.
- teach students how to skim reference material.
- bring in newspaper articles to read to the class.
- occasionally allow partner-reading.

- provide a comfortable reading area with pillows, a rug, a rocker, deck chairs, and a couch.
- practice heterogeneous grouping.
- accept every student as a "member of the literacy club" (Frank Smith 1988).
- use meaningful reading activities instead of worksheets.

Components of My Reading Program

Despite the time crunch of an ever enlarging curriculum, I attempt to spend ninety minutes on reading every day. Here is how I use that precious time.

Modeling

In *Radical Reflections: Passionate Opinions on Teaching, Learning, and Living*, Mem Fox (1993) urges teachers to read where students can see them: "We need to be seen laughing over books, being unable to put books down, sobbing over sob stories, gasping over horror stories, and sighing over love stories—anything, in fact, that helps our students to realize that there is some reward, that there are many rewards, to be had from the act of reading" (63).

Unless I read, how can I convey a love of reading? I join students daily during sustained silent reading. I bring books from home and show them to my students. Fortunately, my mother was an avid reader, and I developed the habit as well. I'd rather read a book than watch television or use the computer. No matter how busy I am, I find time to read. Daniel Pennac, in *Better Than Life* (1994), says, "The issue is not whether or not I have the time to read (after all, no one will ever give me that time), but whether I will allow myself the joy of being a reader" (146–47). I allow myself that joy and my students know it because they see it every day.

Reading Aloud

Daniel Pennac also writes, "A teacher who reads out loud lifts you to the level of books. He gives you the gift of reading!" (111). Each day I read a picture book, a poem, and a section of a novel selected for enjoyment or for its connection to a current study unit. I prefer reading aloud for about fifteen minutes right before lunch and again near the end of the day. I gather the class around me on the rug and read with exaggerated expression. Students' comments and body language reveal their reactions. I make time for this because I want students to feel and think deeply about the book's themes and make connections to our own lives.

My son-in-law, Dale, told me that he still has vivid memories of his sixth-grade teacher reading *Where the Red Fern Grows* by Wilson Rawls. He recalls the entire class weeping together. Oh, the power of words!

For read-alouds, certain authors and books are especially popular with fourth graders. William Steig's books portray universal struggles using a rich array of language. Robert Munsch, the Canadian author, writes funny books that are perfect for choral reading. *The Dragonling*, by Jackie French Zoller, presents the clash between tradition and change. *Mick Harte Was Here*, by Barbara Park, provides a tearful lesson on the importance of wearing a helmet when bike riding. This is just a sampling of my favorites. I am always browsing a local bookstore to find new titles to add to my already lengthy list.

Minilessons

Reading minilessons demonstrate some of the strategies good readers apply and the thinking behind the decisions readers make. I might teach a minilesson about strategies to use when encountering unfamiliar words. Students might use one strategy repeatedly and benefit from knowing other viable ways. I teach minilessons of from ten to forty-five minutes at the overhead. The length depends upon the complexity of strategy and how much student response I elicit. I usually follow this pattern:

- Teach the strategy by modeling.
- Let the students try.
- Review how it went by asking
    1. What problems did you encounter?
    2. What went well?
    3. When will you continue to use the strategy?

I choose topics readers need to know about to be proficient. I may present a minilesson on how to skim a text to gather information for research projects. I give the students a copy of an article and demonstrate the following comprehension strategies (which can also be used in reading fiction):

- Ask questions: ask questions about the story or article.
- Summarize: tell the most important ideas.
- Predict: tell what you think will happen next.
- Clarify: clear up confusion about, for example, what a word means.

Sometimes a minilesson is a five-minute review of a strategy we have already covered. Reviewing encourages students to try it. I come back to some topics more than once:

- my own reading (modeling)
- choosing a book
- book reviews of recent titles
- reading poetry aloud
- skimming reference materials
- what the leader and other members of a literature discussion group do
- good literature discussion questions
- doing choral reading
- using independent reading time wisely
- book interviews

Books I find helpful in developing minilessons include Ellin Oliver Keene and Susan Zimmermann's *Mosaic of Thought: Teaching Comprehension in a Reader's Workshop* and Lucy Calkins, Kate Montgomery, and Donna Santman's *A Teacher's Guide to Standardized Reading Tests: Knowledge Is Power.*

Literature Discussion Groups

I eliminated ability grouping in the mid-1980s because I realized that most students can participate when reading time is focused on discussing and responding. Students "rise to the occasion" when they are viewed as "readers" rather than singled out as unable to read with the rest of the class. My rationale for heterogeneous literature discussion groups is based on what adults do when they read a book: they "discuss" it. The authors of *A Teacher's Guide to Standardized Reading Tests* (1998) say,

> I believe it's by talking about books that children learn to think about books. By retelling a story, children can take the time to build the world of story in their minds. By sharing ideas and by being asked to defend these ideas, children can learn to find evidence from the text to support their theses. (56)

I am always on the lookout for books that lend themselves to in-depth discussion. I select books that have strong characters, such as Patricia MacLachlan's *Sarah, Plain and Tall*, that are full of action and suspense, such as Elvira Woodruff's *Dear Levi*, that show a struggle between friendship and duty, such as Lensey Namioka's *Yang the Youngest and His Terrible Ear*, and others that include literary elements. I divide the class into four groups, which meet simultaneously, and designate a leader for the group. Every student has a turn as leader. During the discussion I move from group to group, making comments and taking notes. I use those notes later for feedback.

I select about six books a year for discussion and we spend approximately three weeks on each book. By reading the same book and assigning pages, every group completes the book at the same time, thus eliminating the problem of keeping one group "on hold" while other groups finish. Groups change for each book, creating new configurations with different dynamics.

In my experience, the same book can serve the needs of both the struggling and the advanced reader. The struggling reader can prepare for the discussion by being paired with a more capable reader, or by working with a student teacher, a parent volunteer, or a tutor. My school district provides tutors in basic skills, who work in my classroom during the language arts block. By using notes about the assigned text, the struggling reader can participate. The advanced reader is usually sufficiently challenged by the high level of discussion that results when the book is good literature.

Before we break into our groups, we talk about the kind of behavior that encourages discussion. For example,

- Everyone will participate.
- We will try not to interrupt each other.
- Nobody will leave the group.
- The group will sit in a circle to allow eye contact.
- Hands will not be raised, as we are having a discussion.
- The leader will keep us on task.
- The leader will select the question and read it aloud.
- It's okay to disagree with one another in a friendly manner.

As students read the assigned pages, they use stick-on notes, as Maryann Eeds and Ralph Peterson (1990) suggest in *Grand Conversations: Literature Groups in Action*, to mark passages they want to talk about, parts they found confusing, or unclear vocabulary. I ask them to jot down a few key words on the stick-on notes to help them recall why they marked the place. These notes usually send students back to the text.

In the past, I wrote open-ended questions for discussion and had students prepare for the discussion by taking notes from the text. But when students met in discussion groups, the conversation was stilted and lacked depth. I wanted to change the format, but I wasn't sure what to substitute for this easily managed system.

Several years ago, when I read *Negotiating the Curriculum*, edited by Garth Boomer, Nancy Lester, Cynthia Onore, and John Cook, it inspired me to involve my students in the decision-making process. I tried asking them for ideas to improve the literature discussion groups. Michael said he thought the discussions were boring. He recommended that students supply the questions and that the groups should read more of the book for the discussion. At first his suggestion made me a little angry. I felt myself becoming defensive. After all, my questions were good. I had been doing it this way for a long time. Visitors to the classroom had commented that they could not distinguish the struggling readers. Yet I heard a small nagging voice in my head saying, "Michael is right. The students don't really care about the content of the discussion. They are going through the motions."

I listened to Michael. For our discussion of the next section of the book, I let the students write their own questions. It was a disaster. Their questions were unbearably literal. At feedback time several students said they liked my questions better. (I must admit I felt some satisfaction.)

I gave the issue more thought. I wasn't going to fall into the trap of trying something new, failing, and giving up. As I thought about what went wrong, I realized that my fourth graders had little experience in writing questions because they were too busy writing answers. I needed to teach them how to write thoughtful questions worth discussing.

Over the next two weeks I asked my students to find questions they thought were good. We considered questions from our social studies text, our weekly newspaper, and those I had written for the reading groups. We talked about what makes a good discussion question.

- Will the question lead to a discussion?
- Can the question be answered by the text?
- Does the question have a connection to another book or to our lives?
- Does the question relate to issues like death, friendship, fear, or other serious topics?

Using these criteria, students reviewed the questions they had asked about the section of text. In small groups, they selected the best questions and carried on lengthy discussions about why a question was or wasn't worth discussing.

Recently, I overheard one group selecting questions for their discussion of *Yang the Youngest and His Terrible Ear*.

"We could combine these two questions."
"I like your wording better. Let's use yours."
"This question has nothing to do with the big meaning of the chapter."
"This is good because it calls for a lot of piggybacking (connecting to someone else's idea)."
"This one touches on what will happen in the next chapter. That's good."

I asked my class how to tell if a question was good. One student volunteered, "A good question is when you think you will have a long discussion about it and can't wait to start talking about it."

I use this process regularly now. After students have selected a few questions in their groups, I combine them all on a sheet to be handed out beforehand. The leader of the literature discussion group chooses questions from the list.

Questions selected for Chapter 2 of *Yang the Youngest and His Terrible Ear*

1. How do you think Matthew felt around Yang's family, being the only one not Chinese?
2. How would you feel if kids made fun of you because you were different?
3. How would you feel if you moved from China to America and didn't know anyone at school? Tell some of the differences between Chinese and American schools.
4. Why do you think Matthew and Yang became good friends?
5. How would you describe Yang's friend, Matthew?
6. Why do you think Yang and Second Sister sit at a table with mostly Asian American people at lunch?
7. Which one do you think you are most like and why: Yang the youngest? Yang the second youngest? Yang the third youngest? Yang the eldest?

Two proposed questions had been eliminated: What did Yang do every time the teacher came into the room? and Why was Second Sister lonely? These were so literal, students thought they wouldn't lead to much discussion.

When students come up with their own discussion questions, they keep questions in mind while they read, a good strategy to develop. When I asked Eliana to reflect on her reading growth, she replied, "I think of questions when I read other books now."

In *Mosaic of Thought* Ellin Oliver Keene and Susan Zimmermann (1997) advocate student-generated questions: "Proficient readers spontaneously generate questions before, during, and after reading." (Because posing questions becomes natural, discussion leaders often ask questions not on the list.) "Proficient readers are aware that as they hear other's questions, new ones are inspired in their own minds" (119).

After twenty minutes, I ask for student comments on each group. Group leaders report, but anyone else in the group can make comments. Negative statements are phrased politely and never directed toward anyone in particular: "We had one person who did not participate" or "We got off the subject," for example. Typical comments are

- Our group had good eye contact.
- We used well-modulated voices (I teach the definition of modulate).
- We referred to the text to support our comments.

- We listened to one another.
- We didn't interrupt each other.
- We piggybacked on each other's comments.
- The leader kept us on the subject.
- Everyone participated in the discussion.

I also offer my observations of the groups I sit with and in doing so reinforce the behavior that support a good discussion. My comments are very specific:

- I like the way Glynae made sure everyone got to speak.
- Scott's group listened to one another.
- Mary's group had excellent eye contact.
- Hannah's group frequently referred to the text to support their opinions.
- Martin politely disagreed with Scott and presented another viewpoint.
- Everyone participated in Rasheed's group.
- There was lots of piggybacking on each other's ideas in Stephen's group.
- Alaina read a quote from the book to explain her thinking.
- I heard Matt say, "I have a connection to my own life."

In advocating discussion groups, Maryann Eeds and Ralph Peterson say, "Participants in dialogue experience in a dramatic way what it means to construct meaning" (1990, 21). In my quest for proficient readers, I am encouraged by the depth of the discussion I hear.

DIRT: *Daily Individual Reading Time*

One Wacky World of DIRT
by Mollie Silver

"DIRT, I can rock 'n' roll around in DIRT, mud pie . . ." This is the theme song that we listen to before we relax and do DIRT (Daily Individual Reading Time). "DIRT" is a time when everyone is in a different world, but all in the same 202 classroom.

After this entertaining song, we sit back and enjoy this VERY IMPORTANT 30 minutes of the day.

When we are reading, if someone finishes a book, they can quickly go to the book spinner full of different worlds. They can choose one to go to and visit.

For example, you can go to a world where 50 stickers are $1.00. Or perhaps you would like to go somewhere where ants find crystals and bring them to their queen. My personal favorite book is T. Margret, and the Rats of Nimh (This is not my only favorite book). It is about rats who find children that are lost and lead them home.

Maybe you like fiction, mysteries, tall tales, or nonfiction. It all depends on what your character is.

As I read, it expands my vocabulary and helps my reading grow. Next year I will probably be humming this song even if we don't have DIRT. I'll always remember the superb times I had reading and traveling to different worlds this year.

DIRT happens every day after lunch. If I skip it, I hear a lot of complaints. Students look forward to this quiet reading period, when they can lounge in comfortable chairs, lean on big pillows, or huddle in corners, totally engrossed in a novel, a magazine, or a beautiful picture book they are sharing with a partner. I, too, read my book of choice.

Sometimes at the end, I ask students to turn to a partner and tell him or her something interesting from their reading. But most of the time we simply savor our moment with our books. Even when I am pushed for time to cover the curriculum, I do not skip DIRT, because I agree with Regie Routman (1991) when she says, "For some students, school is the only place where quiet reading time and the possibility of developing the reading habit is conceivable. Outside of school, video games, videocassette recorders, movies, music, telephone calls, and television often pre-empt what could be time for reading" (42).

The purpose of DIRT is to give students uninterrupted time to read and to practice the reading strategies they have learned. It is essential that the books students select for reading are appropriate for their reading level, so I keep an eye out for students who don't appear to be engaged in their reading or who I know have some reading difficulties. To encourage good matches between book and reader, I provide a wide variety of books in the classroom library and recommend titles in keeping with students' interests and reading level. Struggling readers often get hooked on the Hardy Boys or the Boxcar Children series. The Bailey School Kids books also captivate children who need easier text, and the Encyclopedia Brown series appeals to mystery lovers. Picture books with interesting illustrations and lots of text support slower readers, and because they appear slimmer, they are not so overwhelming. I keep up with children's book publishing to identify titles especially suitable for fourth graders.

Matching the students with books isn't easy. Until students are "hooked on books," it is a struggle to find books that will hold their attention. During DIRT, I often read along with students to get a sense of individual reading ability. As we talk about the book, I can discover whether the student is predicting, making connections to the text, drawing conclusions, and bringing prior knowledge to the text. In these ways, I can judge the appropriateness of that book for that student and identify other titles to recommend.

WEB: *Wonderfully Exciting Books*

Our reading homework is called WEB. In the fall, I define WEB for parents in a letter and enlist their support (Routman 1999).

Dear Families,

WEB (Wonderfully Exciting Books) is an important component of our reading program. The student self-selects books from the classroom, school, public, or home library for independent reading.

Your child will have frequent opportunities to discuss what has been read independently with peers and the teacher. The WEB book will be used for reading at home and may also be used for independent reading during language arts time or during D.I.R.T. (Daily Individual Reading Time). A list of completed books will be kept in the classroom.

Your child's responsibility is to read for about thirty minutes each evening seven days a week, and to carry the book back and forth to school in a waterproof bag. Your child is expected to take good care of this book.

Over the school year, consistent daily reading will expose your child to various authors' styles and will improve your child's fluency, vocabulary, comprehension, and writing. My main goal is that your child will enjoy reading and choose to read for pleasure.

Please join me in helping to create an environment where your children can enjoy books for a lifetime. Together we can build a community of readers.

Thank you for your help, support, and cooperation with our WEB program. Please sign below to indicate that you have read this letter.

Sincerely yours,
Joan Servis

All year the students conduct weekly peer interviews for WEB. The purpose of these interviews is to discuss the book as adults do with friends and to find out about new books they may want to read. When a student finishes reading a book, he puts his name on the board to indicate he is ready for an interview. In a typical interview, two students sit close to one another, with the book between them. Last year my class decided on the following questions as starting points for their conversation:

1. What is the name of the book?
2. Who is the author?
3. What is the book about? Fiction or nonfiction?
4. Tell me something that happened.
5. Do you have a favorite part?
6. Was it easy, hard, or just right (reading level)?
7. Would you recommend the book? Why or why not?

The students keep these questions in their WEB folders to use as a guide. Over the course of the year, students begin to talk to each other more naturally and formal questions become less important (see Figure 5–1).

Each student maintains a log listing the titles of books he or she has read along with the author and genre for each. I look at the logs once a month. Depending on the number of pages and the reading level, some students complete two books a month and others many more. I have kept my own reading log for five years that is identical to the one I ask them to keep, and show it to them. I am hopeful they will continue their logs. The logs are not meant to be a way to check up on them but a way to teach them the value of looking back over their reading to review genres and difficulty levels. A log is also helpful in recalling authors and book recommendations. Most students put an asterisk next to books they highly recommend, as I do. Nick and Stephen devised a system of from one to five stars, five meaning an outstanding book and one meaning so-so.

Last June, for evaluation purposes, I asked the students if they thought the WEB peer interviews were valuable. "I think peer interviews are valuable because they give you a chance to tell someone about the book you have read and maybe recommend it to them," replied Jessica. Kirsten commented: "I think that interviews are valuable because it is kind of like a recommendation and I have

Figure 5–1. A WEB interview

asked people if I can read the book I interviewed them on." Kimberly added, "I would not say valuable but important. They're almost like recommendations because you tell the interviewer all about the book so they want to read it. They also help you organize your thoughts about your book so you know if you like it and what you like about it."

Assessing Reading

My goal in reading assessment is to encourage students to become reflective self-evaluators who are aware of their needs, able to set goals, and able to use appropriate strategies to help themselves become proficient. A student may recognize a need to read aloud with more expression and set that as a goal. Although I am required to assign a letter grade for reading, I find it is difficult to reconcile students' self-assessment and my assessment with letter grades. I employ several evaluative tasks, forms, and observations to achieve a better balance.

Benchmark Reading Tests

"Benchmark books" are books that have been selected by a committee of teachers in my district as examples of what a student should be able to read independently at a given grade. Each trimester I devise a "benchmark" test using a fourth-grade book unfamiliar to students. In class I ask students to read the book individually. Then I give the test, which asks questions about the text. I allow them to refer to their books. Most of the questions are literal, since I want to determine not only if they can read the material but if they can find answers in the text (not unlike state-mandated tests).

The test for *How the Forest Grew*, by William Jaspersohn, was as follows:

Directions: Answer the question in a complete sentence using words from the question.

1. Most forests have three stages of growth. What are they?
2. A full-grown forest has five layers. What are they?
3. What does counting a tree's growth rings tell you?
4. What are fungi?
5. What are signs of animal life in a forest? Name five.
6. Name three poisonous plants found in a forest.
7. What does it mean to "girdle" a tree?
8. Why shouldn't you pull the bark off a tree?
9. Why shouldn't you eat berries or mushrooms from the forest?
10. Name some birds that live in a forest.
11. What is humus?
12. What is "succession" in a forest?

I give students as much time as they need, since I am not testing for reading speed but for reading comprehension. If a student cannot read the fourth-grade benchmark book, I do a one-on-one running record using books at a second- and third-grade level. Taking a running record consists of having a student read an identified passage while I record miscues and analyze them later. Doing one allows me to assess the child's oral reading, by analyzing miscues or strategies used. I might also ask the child to tell me the content orally, in order to check her understanding of the meaning. The child retells the information stated directly in the text and what she has inferred from her reading. The benchmark books, running records, and oral retellings enable me to tailor my assessment to each student's reading level and individual difficulties.

Reading Logs

I check the WEB reading logs for two reasons: to note whether the student is reading regularly and independently and to ensure that the student is reading in a variety of genres. If I think a student should be completing more books, I meet with him to discuss the problem. I may also encourage the student to select a book in a genre he hasn't tried, but I do not insist because the choice is his. I ensure that students encounter many different kinds of texts through reading aloud and the books I select for reading discussion groups, so I am not overly concerned if a student focuses on a particular genre (see Figure 5–2).

Rubrics

My colleagues and I compiled a reading rubric, but we found it difficult to use because some of the indicators, such as "makes relevant contributions," were ambiguous. I wanted a rubric the students and I could use, one that incorporated child-friendly language and listed reasonable criteria for evaluation. Because I put such emphasis on student self-assessment, it was especially important that students could use it easily to evaluate their own progress, so I asked them to help me design a rubric for our November parent conferences. In our discussions, we referred to the district report card to make sure we included all important areas. Then we selected the indicators by vote, and now we use this rubric each trimester. Students also refer to it in filling out self-evaluation forms for the November and March parent conferences (see Figures 5–3 and 5–4).

Observations

During reading discussion groups, I observe students as they offer comments, ask questions, listen to each other, make points, follow along, and refer to the book. I also take notes, which I keep for reference. This enables me to assess students more accurately and fairly.

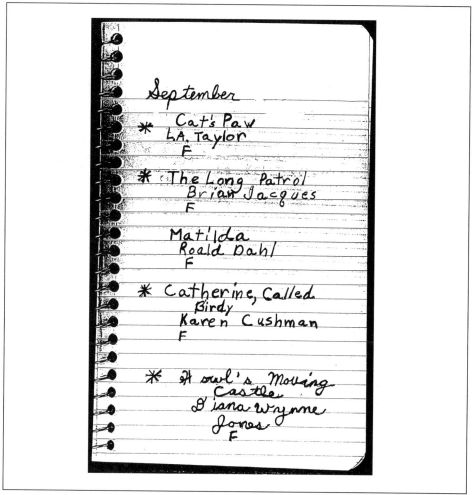

Figure 5–2. A page in a student reading log

Narratives

My students write narrative summaries of their accomplishments for the June report cards. Here are self-assessments by Andrew, Jenna, and Anna, written in third person:

Andrew's Narrative

His favorite books are *Hatchet* and *The River* both by Gary Paulson. He gladly accepts classmates recommendations on good books. Andrew, voracious reader has recently finished a 400+ page guide to the Universe.

Name Jenny	Date 11–11		

Reading Assessment Rubric—Written by 4th Graders

Indicators	Usually	Rarely	Evidence
Independent Reading			
1. Chooses appropriate books (just right or challenging)	✓		The Chaos Gate
2. Chooses to read	✓		My log
3. Reads part of book to see if likes it—takes recommendations	✓		
4. Chooses variety of genre		✓	I almost always read fiction
5. Predicts what will happen	✓		
To Understand Book: Uses Strategies			
1. Connects to life or other books		✓	
2. Rereads for meaning	✓		
3. Substitutes—skips unknown words	✓		
4. Reads whole sentence to get meaning when don't know word	✓		
5. Can tell what is happening in book —can retell	✓		Reading Benchmark
In Literature Discussion Groups			
1. Makes comments	✓		
2. Asks questions	✓		
3. Listens to others	✓		
4. Makes point—disagrees	✓		
5. Follows along	✓		
6. Refers to book	✓		
Non Fiction Research			
1. Finds right books		✓	
2. Skims books for information	✓		
3. Perseveres	✓		
Aloud			
1. Reads fluently with expression		✓	

Figure 5–3. Jenny's completed reading assessment rubric

Andrew will reread a sentence to find a definition to an unknown word. If he can't find the definition, he will look it up in the dictionary. He will determinedly read a long book to it's finish.

Andrew will readily participate in literature discussion groups. He will listen to whomsoever's talking. Andrew will also try to watch the speaker.

Andrew will read at the least, one hour almost every night.

Name: Julia

Subject: reading

What I can do well.	What I find hard.
I can find a book very well. I look at things that interest me, not others. I read alot, but not all good readers read all the time, I read when I want and I think thats good. Most of the time I can figure out words. I like or love books.	What I find hard is when tha Author puts the sentence in a odd way, I have to read it over a billion times. I also find it hard when I can't spell or say the word so it does not make sense.

What I am doing better.	What I am going to work on next.
I am doing alot better at picking out books I want, like books from Karen Hesse or Sharen Creech. Not picking out books that I think is junk very soon like in the second chapter	I am going to work on finishing books. I start a book and then I never finish it, I then move on to a-nother book.

Figure 5–4. Julia's reading self-assessment

Jenna's Narrative

Jenna is an excellent reader who challenges herself to hard books like *Dogsong* by Gary Paulson and *Jacob Have I Loved* by Katherine Paterson. Like any other fourth grader, Jenna reads about one to two hours every day. She reads in quiet places like her room, the library and down in the basement. She asks librarians, even teachers, their recommendations for good books.

One of her favorite books is *This Island Isn't Big Enough for the Four of Us* by Gary Greer and Bob Runkin. Also, she enjoys *Hatchet* by Gary Paulson.

Jenna likes reading discussion group. She always gives her opinion. She is trying not to talk so loudly. Some strategies she uses are if she is reading hard books, she will read it to her Mom, sound out the word or ask her mom and dad. Then she'll look it up in her spell checker.

Jenna is a slow reader but she's getting faster. Jenna's goal is to stick with a book even if she is having trouble. She also is going to keep a notebook for the summer.

Anna's Narrative

"Turn off the light!"

"One more chapter," Anna enjoys reading a lot. She is frequently reading *Wait Till Helen Comes* by Mary Hahn. She is fond of the following authors: Roald Dahl, E.B. White, and Jan Greenberg.

When she comes to a sentence or phrase or even a word that she finds hard to understand, Anna uses these strategies: Breaks it into chunks, reads it over 3 times or just skips it.

She reads with magnificent expression while reading aloud.

In reading discussion group this kid overflows with spectacular ideas. She shares them so that she doesn't burst.

Because we engage in informal self-assessment all year, students can describe themselves fairly accurately. And parents like these narratives because they receive more information from them than they do from a single letter grade.

In determining letter grades, I consider students' self-assessments. These are a valuable source of information on how they approach and solve a problem, such as how and why they select certain books for independent reading, their participation in discussion groups, and areas in which they want to improve. The final grade is based on all the data I have gathered using these assessment tools. While I don't claim that these tools are perfect, I am constantly revising the rubrics, rethinking tests, and making changes. As Lucy Calkins and her colleagues (1998) say, "All of us, given the opportunity, will have insights into improving our teaching. All of us have strengths to build on, weaknesses to shore up, changes to make, and higher goals to reach. This seems to be both the burden and thrill of our profession. There is always a new horizon just over the next hill-top" (64).

Years in the future, if current trends continue, I expect to see my former students at neighborhood bookstores on Friday evenings. I'll bump into them, browsing through the aisles, drinking coffee and tea, and listening to pleasant music. I'm hopeful that they will have stacks of books waiting to be read next to their beds and shelves lined with books they have read and return to often. I'd like to think that I have helped them on the way to becoming thoughtful adults.

6

Success in Mathematics

My students like mathematics because they enjoy interacting with each other while solving problems. In fact, after an afternoon of working intensely with her team on attribute-block problems, a new student in my class said, "Mrs. Servis. The day is so short in this class!"

What Does My Math Class Look Like and Why?

My math class has changed over the years. Gone are the endless worksheets and the repetitious copying of pages in the math textbook. Now students have conversations about math. In pairs or teams of four they work with manipulatives, such as attribute blocks, which come in different colors, shapes, and sizes, and are used to explore logical thinking. I sit with them, talking about math problems. A student may offer to demonstrate how she solved a problem on the overhead so the entire class can follow her thinking. In this way, students discover that there is often more than one way to solve a problem. I find it fascinating to discover all the different ways children think about the same thing. In this chapter I will elaborate on my move away from the traditional algorithm approach, which can result in proficiency but not always in understanding.

My Students Solve Problems Together

In 1980 I took courses at Cleveland State University sponsored by the Carnegie Corporation of New York. Entitled "Equals," these courses promoted group work through "hands-on" experiences in logical thinking and problem solving, with a special emphasis on closing the math performance gap between males and females. I realized that I needed to change my practice to benefit my students.

As I moved from being a traditional, "by the book" teacher to one who is more reflective, I also needed to bring individual students, working on textbook problems in isolation, together into a mathematical community of learners. I didn't want to be viewed as the only authority.

Through talking, the students maintain a community: they show respect to one another and they listen to one another. At the same time, as Rebecca B. Corwin, Judith Storeygard, and Sabra L. Price point out in *Talking Mathematics: Supporting Children's Voices,*

> Participating in mathematical conversations is central to developing strong mathe-matical ideas. Talking allows students to compare their methods and discuss their ideas and theories with their classmates. Classmates' questions or counter asser-tions often force a student to examine her own mathematical concept and ideas. When students begin to comment on each other's methods and ask each other questions, confusion is clarified. (1996, 2)

During class, students practice implementing a concept I have introduced by col-loborating on problems. In small groups they pool their strategies to find solu-tions. Conversation is a way to clarify thinking that also makes every student in the group a resource in figuring out procedures. When a small group has mastered the concept, I give them more difficult problems that require them to apply what they have learned. Success builds confidence that they can apply their under-standing of mathematical principles to new situations.

My Students Use Manipulatives

Math manipulatives can be moved around and arranged in different combina-tions so that students can "see" the solution to a problem. In geometry, for exam-ple, students use Geoboards with rubber bands to divide figures into congruent parts. Because manipulating the rubber bands makes it easy to try out different ways of defining space, they use the Geoboards eagerly, gaining practice with the concept of congruence.

My colleague Kristi Roberts had her class build a model of a cube with tooth-picks and miniature marshmallows to illustrate intersecting parallel and perpen-dicular lines. When they had completed their cubes, Kristi asked students to label with masking tape five things on their model that are always true about a cube, using geometric terms. Andrea labeled her model "polyhedron," "eight ver-tices," "twelve edges," "special rectangular prism," and "parallel edges." When Kristi asked her about the definition of a special rectangular prism, she said, "A cube is a rectangular prism because all the sides are square."

Manipulatives capitalize on visual thinking to reinforce retention. They give concrete meaning to mathematical ideas, which is especially helpful to students who have difficulty understanding abstract symbols.

Traditional paper-and-pencil methods encourage rote memorization. But when students represent an algorithm concretely, using manipulatives, they find it easier to apply it in practical, everyday situations. For example, the algorithm for finding the area of a square is $A = L \times W$. By using tiles to fill up the designated area, the student "sees" that the area is the product of length times width.

I Pay Attention to Gender Differences

In September, it is not uncommon to hear fourth-grade girls express "math anxiety" or a fear of not doing well. They say, "I don't like math" or "I'm not good at math." Even when girls know the answers, they tend not to volunteer them. Boys are slower to share their thinking. They want to give the answers rather than explain how they got them.

As the NCTM's Professional Teaching Standards points out, "current work indicates that females make sense of information and learn in ways that are significantly different from the traditional approach to teaching mathematics." I asked our district math consultant, Judy Wells, if she noticed any differences between girls and boys in math classes. "Yes," she said. "Gender is a factor in fourth and fifth grade. Boys are generally more competitive and aggressive. Girls are more cooperative and want to talk about math."

She also told me, however, in that classrooms where teachers nurture mathematical discourse, a verbal exchange of ideas, the differences disappear. In *Feisty Females: Inspiring Girls to Think Mathematically*, Karen Karp and her colleagues (1998) state, "Students, particularly females, need to openly talk about their discoveries and listen and react to the thinking of others" (19). Encouraging everyone, boys and girls, to demonstrate their thinking at the overhead helps them feel that their ideas are valid and worthwhile. An atmosphere of mutual respect lessens competition and fosters confidence, which benefits everyone but is especially needed by some girls.

How Do I Plan My Mathematics Teaching?

My school district requires that certain mathematical strands or major concepts be taught in the fourth grade. I use the mathematics textbook only as a supplemental resource, plugging parts of it into the mathematical strands I teach, so I devise a teaching plan for the year that incorporates a number of resources. Having a plan, including a list of lessons and resources, lets me focus on a concept in depth and teach it in a variety of ways. I don't need to rely on the textbook as a curriculum guide or spend time hunting for a lesson the day I need it. I know where to look by referring to my plan.

Organizing the Year

Making the initial time outline for teaching all the mathematical strands was a big undertaking. I had to decide how much time to spend on each major concept and when to teach it. For example, I decided to teach the geometry strand first, because our use of manipulatives and group work would help build community at the beginning of the year.

I revise my outline every year, adding and deleting resources and ideas. Here is a sample:

1. August 27
    Major: Data / Geometry
    Minor: Review of addition and subtraction facts with extensions (10 or 15 minutes daily, or one day a week)
2. October 20
    Major: Place Value
    Minor: Review basic facts of multiplication and division with extensions
    Mental Math
3. November 17
    Major: Fractions: Cover concept of fractions: equivalent, comparing, addition, and subtraction
    Minor: Computation of addition and subtraction (adding) 3- and 4-digit numbers
4. January 5
    Major: Problem Solving / Averaging
    Minor: Multiplication by One Number
5. January 26
    Major: Division
6. February 17
    Major: Linear Measurement
    Minor: Patterns
7. March 9
    Major: Multiplication with Two Digits
8. April 6
    Major: Time and Money
9. May 4
    Major: Decimals
10. May 26
    Major: Algebra
    Students learn to use calculators throughout the year.

Listing topics as "major" and "minor" refers not to importance but to emphasis. The minor topics are primarily for review: On October 20, for example, we spent most of our math period learning and revising place value and then reviewed basic multiplication and division facts. Under each strand, I list possible lessons and the books I could use in teaching it.

Strand 3: Fractions
    Textbook: Chapter 8
    Possible lessons:
1. Carton Fractions: Lesson 50, *Math in the Mind's Eye*
2. Fraction Factory Activities (folder)
3. Fraction Bars: Textbook, p. 246
    Teach game: "Flip"
4. Fraction No Match (folder)
5. Fraction Addition: *Connections*, p. 48
6. It's in the Lowest Terms (folder)
7. Textbook: pp. 250–251
8. Equivalent Fractions: *Connections*, pp. 44–45
9. Fraction Puzzles with Pattern Blocks (Cooperative Learning folders)
10. Fractions on the Geoboard (small booklet in folder)
11. Fraction Bars: Lesson 54, *Math in the Mind's Eye*
12. Equivalent Fractions: Lesson 55, *Math in the Mind's Eye*
13. *About Teaching Mathematics*: Fractions, pp. 212–225

When I outline possible lessons for each strand, I do not list them in the order in which I would teach them, nor do I intend to use all of them. I simply go through all my materials and list those most appropriate for each strand.

The folders contain lessons I've collected or pulled out of books; all are filed alphabetically. *Math in the Mind's Eye*, available from Portland State University in Oregon, features lessons from the Visual Mathematics Courses. I have about eighty lessons for fourth through sixth grade. *Connections* by Micaelia Randolph Brummett and colleagues (1989), which the district provides, is a resource for teaching fractions, place value, patterns and numbers, geometric thinking and measurement, and decimals.

Beginning teachers often lack resources. I have a few suggestions:

- Ask a veteran teacher to share resources and ideas.
- Ask your district to purchase math resources.
- Spend your own money to buy resources.

My colleague Anika Simpson tells me, "I was able to follow your math plan [which I shared with her] by raiding your file cabinet my first year."

Of course, I don't follow this plan rigidly. In order to expose students to decimals before the state-mandated test in March, for example, I teach a few lessons on decimals earlier than the schedule suggests. I also adjust my plans to include new materials. Judy Wells, our district math coach, often gives me books she feels are good resources. I replace scheduled lessons with alternatives temporarily, and only make a permanent change when I've gauged their effectiveness and the students' enthusiasm.

Individualizing Instruction

Accommodating the wide range of abilities in a math class can be difficult. When I took a series of workshops and seminars that involved the same kind of active participation I require of my students, I became more aware of the variety of learning styles within one classroom. I was slower to grasp concepts than some of my teammates. I needed more time to think about what I was going to do. I became frustrated when partners went ahead without me. I keep this experience in mind in planning lessons. When we work in pairs, I put students of similar ability together. Some exceptional math students have difficulty explaining their thinking to others because their minds work so rapidly. Other students ask to work alone, and I occasionally provide opportunities.

For students who need the challenge of stretching their thinking beyond the basic concept, I offer extensions. If, for example, the basic lesson asked students to make up word problems that can be solved using a map from Joan Westley's (1994) *Puddle Questions: Assessing Mathematical Thinking*, the extension might have pairs of students creating their own hiking maps of imaginary parks. The students would draw the trails to scale, labeling special sites and recording mileage for the trails. I like resources that provide extensions (and list several at the end of this chapter). I also keep a shelf of math games for reinforcement and enrichment.

A Typical Lesson

When I teach mixed numbers for fractions, I use a folder titled "Sharing Cookies." I learned about the activity at a workshop, and it can be found in Marilyn Burns' (1992) *About Teaching Mathematics*. The problem: "Divide 7 cookies equally among four friends. Write out how you solved the problem in your math spiral."

I begin the lesson by reading *The Doorbell Rang* by Pat Hutchins, a story about a group of children who have to share their cookies. It inspires discussion about dividing a batch of cookies and creates interest in our problem.

Dividing the students into groups of four, I present the problem and pass out the materials: each group receives seven paper circles representing cookies. All they need is paper, rulers, and pencils. As students investigate, there is lots of conversation, cutting, and experimenting. If one group completes the task, I have other, similar tasks they can try (such as dividing three cookies equally among five friends).

After about thirty minutes, I call the class back together and ask for a spokesperson from each group, although each member must be capable of explaining the group's thinking to ensure that no one student dominates. Each spokesperson demonstrates the group's answer on the overhead, drawing the cookies and showing how to divide them. Usually, students have arrived at the same answers but in different ways. Some have divided six cookies into halves and the seventh into fourths, as Joey's write-up illustrates. Other groups have divided all seven cookies into fourths and made four piles of fourths (see Figure 6–1).

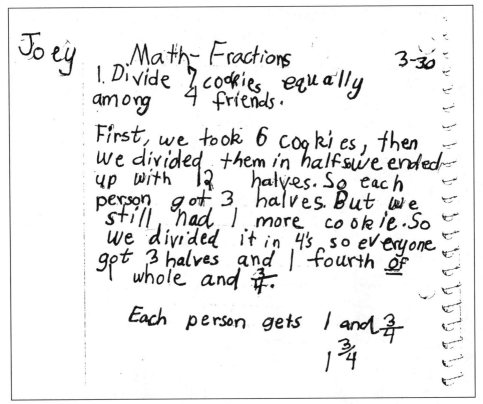

Figure 6–1. Joey wrote about dividing cookies

We talk about the results as a group and come to some conclusions: We note the importance of being accurate in creating halves and fourths. We use fractional language, representing the fractions with standard symbols. We define the terms "equivalent," "denominator," and "numerator." Visual representations and a concluding discussion help students clarify their thinking.

Homework can be a variation on this problem so students can practice the strategies: for example, divide four pizzas equally among nine friends.

How Do I Assess Students?

Students' homework, participation in classroom discussions, and my observation of students' reasoning processes during group work are important factors in my daily assessment of their mathematical understanding. Less frequently, I also use quizzes, tests, students' written descriptions of their thinking, group evaluation forms, individual performance testing, and rubrics. The final grade is based on the results of several procedures.

Homework

I assign math homework daily, using primarily the textbook and assignments from Julie Pier Brodie and colleagues (1996) *Mathland: Journeys Through Mathematics: Daily Tune-Ups 2*. The problems are basic, but I also require students to explain their thinking in solving the problems (see Figure 6–2).

To the six talented math students in her fourth-grade class, Julie Beers assigns a weekly problem-solving packet in addition to their regular math homework. The packet contains seven challenging problems to be completed by Friday.

In grading daily homework assignments I give either a check (satisfactory) or a check minus (the paper needs work). Students make corrections and resubmit. This system works well. If a student's assignment contains numerous errors, I meet with that student to review the concept.

Observations

During classroom discussions and group work, I take notes about students' contributions. I also recognize whether the student reasons logically: Is the student confused about the sequence of steps? Can the student use a particular algorithm with a reasonable degree of proficiency? Does the student attempt to make sense of the problem? Can the student explain his thinking? I record my observations in a notebook designated for math and refer to it when I talk to parents and when I'm doing evaluations. I write my observations down during

Figure 6–2. Alaina's explanation of her thinking

planning periods and after school, when I have time for reflection. During math class I'm often too busy working with students. I find it difficult. My intentions are good, but time is often in short supply. Each year I vow to do better.

Quizzes

Although I focus on the process of mathematical thinking, memorization also has a place in my classroom. Students who memorize have quicker access to math facts for more complicated processes, such as long division. I give quizzes on facts once every two weeks or so; I file them to note improvements but do not grade them. My intent is simply to emphasize the usefulness of this kind of mental "databank." Every so often I give a short quiz on a new concept, such as double-digit multiplication, to evaluate students' understanding of the approach I have used.

Tests

At the end of a unit of study, I give a test, usually a short-answer test with problems similar to those covered in the unit. If a grade is low, students can retake the test. Beforehand, we meet to attempt to find out what is confusing them. Then I reteach the concept. The students and I brown-bag it, since often the only time I can squeeze in for reteaching is during lunch. Sometimes I try a different approach and sometimes I go over the previous classwork, whichever seems more likely to promote understanding. I give the student a study guide and, in a few days, a second test with similar problems. I record the second grade. I want students to demonstrate that they understand the concept.

Periodically I give performance task tests based on completed work. In geometry, for example, I might ask questions like the following:

1. Using a Geoboard and a rubber band, make a triangle. Divide the triangle in half. Are the two triangles congruent? Represent your Geoboard on the Geoboard paper.
2. Make a parallelogram on your Geoboard. Draw it on the Geoboard paper.
3. Make a quadrilateral polygon on your Geoboard. Draw it on the Geoboard paper.
4. Define and draw an obtuse angle.
5. Choose a manipulative and using mathematical language, write about the manipulative to illustrate your understanding of geometric terms.

Writing About Their Thinking

Lynn Arthur Steen (1989), who teaches mathematics at St. Olaf College, says that "There is no better way to learn mathematics than by working in groups, by teaching mathematics to one another, by arguing about strategies, and by expressing arguments carefully in written form." Students in my class must explain the thinking they have used in solving a problem. When Kristi Roberts' students constructed a cube using marshmallows and toothpicks, she asked them to explain their thinking process in writing using geometric terminology (see Figure 6–3).

If students have difficulty putting their ideas into writing in September, it becomes easier for them as the year progresses. I agree with Karen Karp and her colleagues (1998): "With time and experience, good modeling by the teacher, peer conferencing by other students, and reading aloud works of others, students gain confidence in their own writing" (22). I do not grade mathematical explanations, but I do make comments and sometimes ask for further details.

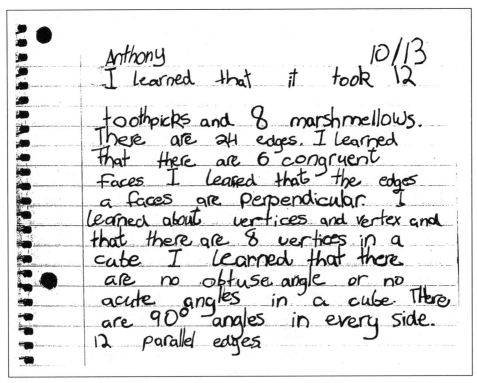

Figure 6–3. Anthony's written explanation of his thinking

According to the NCTE (1989) *Curriculum and Evaluation Standards for School Mathematics*, "The assessment of students' mathematical knowledge should yield information about their ability to use mathematical language to communicate ideas" (205).

Forms of Self-Evaluation

I expect my students to reflect on their progress. Some of the methods I use are

Group Evaluation: I usually ask a series of questions to elicit the students' sense of the group's effort:

- Was your group on task?
- What did you contribute to the team?
- What will we you do better next time?
- What was easy for you during this lesson?
- What was hard for you during this lesson?

Glynae, Mike, Eli, and Stephen worked together on a problem-solving lesson about sharing money. Afterward, they evaluated their performance as a team (see Figure 6–4). Most days, however, evaluation consists of a simple question at the end of a lesson: "What was something you did particularly well in your group?"

Narratives: At March conference time, I ask students to summarize their individual progress in a short narrative. Jessica, writing about herself in the third person, said this:

> In math Jessica is improving. She constantly uses math vocabulary. She is working on memorizing multiplication facts. She picked up long division with ease.
>
> Jessica is especially good in fractions. She also enjoys working with shapes.
>
> Jessica volunteers ideas orally in class and is working hard in class proving her answers. She enjoys listening to others' ideas so she can respond and either agree or disagree in a polite manner.
>
> One of Jessica's strengths is writing in her math spiral. Her writing reflects thought and is very detailed. She works well in a group and contributes her ideas to form a solution.

The only assistance students need for these narratives is a brainstorming session beforehand to remind them of what we value in math class.

Rubrics: The fourth-grade teaching team—Julie Beers, Kristi Roberts, Anika Simpson, and I—designed a math rubric listing our expectations for our students.

Names **Glynae, Mike, Eli, Stephen**   Date **2-25**

_____

Group Evaluation
Lesson: Sharing Money

1. We rate our group (an excellent, a good, a fair, a poor) team, because...

   We rated our group an excellent because everybody had something to do and we weren't too loud so other groups couldn't concintrate.

2. This is what was easy for us during this lesson.

   What was easy for our group was we all worked together as a team and we all agreed on what we were going to do and even if someone didn't agree we worked it out so everyone was happy on what job they had.

3. This is what was hard for us during this lesson.

   What was hard was at first we couldn't agree what job to pick and we also had a little trouble with the $.50 problem.

Figure 6–4. Group Evaluation

Indicators

- communicates using mathematical language and forms (diagrams, pictures, talk, writing)
- is inquisitive, reflective, and self-directed
- meets classroom and homework expectations
- demonstrates understanding of mathematical concepts

- is accurate and complete
- demonstrates persistence (keeps trying)
- uses appropriate materials and strategies
- makes connections among math topics
- uses a variety of strategies in problem-solving situations
- checks work over carefully

We asked the students to rate themselves for each item on a scale of 1 to 10, 10 being the best.

Included on the rubric were some additional points:

- what I do well in math
- what I like about math
- what I find hard about math
- what I dislike about math

Most revealing were student responses to these points. Several said it was hard to write about math. Most commented that they liked working in groups with manipulatives on problem-solving activities. The students showed the rubric to parents at the student-led conferences (described in Chapter 8).

The rubric needs rewriting to use more child-friendly language, and I plan to ask students to help in the revision.

Math class is one of my favorite parts of the school day. I no longer worry about whether I can meet the needs of the student struggling to understand a new concept and of the exceptional student looking for a challenge. Students are totally engaged. It is rare for anyone to be off task, because using manipulatives, solving problems, and having the opportunity to talk and work with others is enjoyable. The tasks are usually challenging, not tedious, and capture students' interest.

Through teamwork, students are solving problems. They function as a community with common goals. They participate actively in their own learning, instead of receiving knowledge passively. Their confidence soars when they succeed in a subject viewed as difficult. Their anxiety drops, and they begin to enjoy mathematics.

Math proficiency is necessary in many careers, so I am determined to nurture this positive view by minimizing the fear of failure and including every student as an equal and active participant. Here are some of my favorite math resources.

About Teaching Mathematics: A K–8 Resource, by Marilyn Burns

Provides problem-solving activities in the strands of measurement, probability and statistics, geometry, logic, patterns and functions, and numbers. Also has suggestions for teaching place value, multiplication, division, fractions, decimals, percentages, addition, and subtraction. Easy to read and use.

A Collection of Math Lessons from Grades 3 Through 6, by Marilyn Burns

Very easy to use, in scripted form, with rationale for each approach.

Math at a Glance: A Month-by-Month Celebration of the Numbers Around Us, by Susan Ohanian

Mathematical investigations for each month that make connections to language arts, geography, science, art, music, and sports.

Math for Girls and Other Problem Solvers, by Diane Downie, Twila Slesnick, and Jean Kerr Stenmark

Problem-solving activities include games and puzzles, providing fun and increasing lasting interest in mathematics. The activities are appropriate for both boys and girls, but they were designed to stimulate curiosity and interest in mathematics in students who thought of math as scary or boring. Very easy to implement.

Mathland: Journeys Through Mathematics: Daily Tune-Ups 2, by Julie Pier Brodie, Rhea Irvine, Cynthia Reah, Ann Roper, Kelly Stewart, and Kathryn Walker

Reproducible activities for homework, arithmetic, and test practice. The best part of this book is the "Convince Me!" approach to computational problem solving. It relies on logical discussion and number sense, and helps students write about their thinking. Students record their solution to the problem and the thinking they used to solve it. What they write should convince others that their answer is correct.

Puddle Questions: Assessing Mathematical Thinking, by Joan Westley

Blackline masters for open-ended problems to solve in groups. Assessment criteria are listed and detailed prompts for teachers. Each problem will take one class period.

S.P.A.C.E.S. Solving Problems of Access to Careers in Engineering and Science, developed by Lawrence Hall of Science, Berkeley

Projects give students experience in developing logical reasoning and problem-solving skills. Excellent source of extension activities, which usually last over a three- or four-day period.

Wollygoggles and Other Creatures, by Thomas C. O'Brien

Problems designed for small groups, with three levels of difficulty: easy, medium, and hard.

New materials are published every year. Heinemann, Cuisenaire, Dale Seymour, and Creative Publications issue periodic catalogs of recent publications.

7

Implementing Science and Social Studies

For the content areas, teachers receive curriculum guides and textbooks designating specific units for each grade. For fourth grade, my district focuses on the regions of the United States in social studies and on land and water biomes, weather, and sound in science. I've been teaching for a long time. Do I disregard the district mandates and let units evolve according to my students' interests? Do all my content-area topics dovetail into one common theme because I'm a holistic teacher? How much choice do I give students? These are the questions I'll attempt to answer in this chapter.

What Is Important

As important as these questions are, what is vital to me is whether in *implementing* the science and social studies curriculum I'm true to my beliefs about how children learn best. I believe optimum learning occurs in classrooms where students talk, work in teams, collaborate, applaud, reflect, respond, and perform authentic tasks. They ask questions and find answers. Students will need to know how to gather information and do research as they progress through school and as they move on into careers and adult lives. They may forget facts and figures: the important thing is that they know how to locate information.

I comply with the required units of study, hoping the educators who have developed them are focusing on the "bigger picture" (K–12 sequence). But I do more. By emphasizing the inquiry process, I am able to teach any unit mandated by the district in a more meaningful and productive way. I've also joined curriculum committees to help design the units I will be teaching. In most school districts today, teachers are invited to help create curriculum guides or select textbooks.

Many excellent books are available to assist teachers in enriching content-area lessons, so here, I will focus on how my beliefs look in action.

Preparing a Unit

Sticking to the prescribed fourth-grade social studies and science units doesn't mean I can't decide how to implement the units. As I approach a unit of study I think about the global concepts, the connections between ourselves and the world. I want my students to think about why we are covering this unit. I might ask, "Why should we learn about Ohio?" We brainstorm together and I would record their reasons on the chalkboard:

- We live in Ohio.
- We can visit places in Ohio.
- Materials for research are easy to get.
- Ohio is an important state with some big cities.
- We will have questions about Ohio on the proficiency test.
- Ohio is a part of the woodlands biome (which we study in science).

Jo-Anne Reid (1992), reflecting on her experience in the classroom, concludes: "For students to become involved in the learning process, there seems only one necessity: that they perceive a sense of purpose in what they are doing" (117). Asking my students why we study a topic encourages a shared sense of purpose.

What We Know

My students come to fourth grade already knowing a lot about a topic. One collects rocks, another goes on weekend shoots with her photographer father, still another is fascinated by sharks. I look for possible "experts," students who have a particular interest in a particular topic and have become very knowledgeable about it. "Experts" bring books, artifacts, and a sense of enthusiasm to the subject, and we all learn from them. I never assume that each year's students have the same knowledge.

To find out what we already know, we divide into small groups to generate information about the subject we're going to study. After about fifteen minutes we regroup and put our discoveries on the chalkboard or the overhead. When we studied sound in science, we came up with this list:

- Sound travels in waves.
- The longer the sound wave the lower the sound.
- Different objects make different sounds.

- Sound is everywhere.
- There are some sounds humans can't hear.
- Some objects sound the same.
- Bats use sound to locate things.
- Ear infections cause hearing problems.
- The shorter the sound wave the higher the sound.

In this way, I can prepare lessons that build on these foundations. At the end of the unit, I revisit this list with the class to show them how much they have learned.

What We Want to Know

Another way to learn about students' interests and involve them in unit planning is to ask them what they *want* to know. I gather nonfiction books on the topic we're investigating from the school or the public library, spread them out on the tables, and invite students in small groups to think of questions. After about thirty minutes I ask each group to share their questions as I write them down on chart paper. When we began our study of the prairie, students generated the following list (with my assistance in wording).

1. How many Native American tribes are there? Name them.
2. What different kinds of people live on the prairie?
3. What are some of the traditions of the different tribes of Native Americans?
4. What is the largest prairie state? Smallest?
5. How many prairie states are there and what are their names?
6. What plants grow on the prairie besides grasses?
7. What are some of the most common animals on the prairie?
8. What other biomes in the world are similar to the U.S. prairie?
9. Do some prairie animals live in other biomes? What are they?
10. How is the prairie different from where we live?
11. Are there any famous people from the prairie? Who are they?
12. What wars were fought on the prairie?
13. Which prairie territories first became states?
14. Who were the first settlers of the prairie after the Native Americans?

The questions helped us select topics for role-playing speeches. Michael, for example, portraying a Sioux Indian chief, gave us lots of information about the tribe. These questions could also have been used as research topics for written or oral reports.

Gathering Information

I make sure there are enough books and other source materials in the classroom from which students can take notes for their specific area of research.

Using All Kinds of Sources

My students and I discuss where we might obtain information for our unit study. They suggest the usual resources: nonfiction books, encyclopedias, magazines, videos, field trips, newspaper articles, and the Internet. For many years I have been collecting newspaper clippings. With funds given to teachers for classroom materials, I also buy books about our topics. Library book sales are another source of nonfiction books, and often parents will send in videos and printouts of Internet research.

Sometimes students go straight to the source. For the unit on Ohio, they "adopted" Ohio cities and wrote business letters to representatives requesting information. By creating a bulletin board on Ohio cities, posting the materials, and displaying a note card of facts about each city, students could take a personal interest in "their" city. They also planned trips to each "adopted" city with their parents.

We try to bring in speakers from the community. When we were researching Native Americans, the fourth-grade team invited a member of the Apache tribe to talk to our students. He told us that Native Americans do not like to be called "redskins" because the term originated during a period in our history when a bounty was paid for a piece of "red" skin removed from a Native American. He shared his children's unhappiness when their classmates dress up like warriors to represent Native Americans at Thanksgiving and Halloween. Looking at history from his perspective caused students to think about stereotyping and about historical events not covered in our textbook. The visit provoked an interesting discussion about point of view and whether we should believe everything we read.

Taking Notes

Teaching students how to take notes eliminates the problem of direct word-for-word copying from books and computer printouts. In the fall, before the class begins any research, we review note-taking skills. Students need to know how to skim material, how to summarize, and how to record facts in their own words. To demonstrate, I use the social studies textbook or a magazine article in a direct note-taking lesson. At the overhead, I read aloud a paragraph from a transparency of an article, telling the students I am searching for facts. I state what I think is important and then write it down on the transparency in my own words.

I continue like this through the article, thinking aloud, pulling out the facts I want to remember, and recording them. I repeat the process with a different article or a selection from a book, asking the students to record the facts we select as a group on notebook paper. Over several days, I repeat the process, gradually giving less help until the students are taking notes independently.

When I think they are adept at notetaking I challenge them to prove that their notes are adequate by using them to write a brief report. But first I collect the notes and hold them for two weeks. Then I pass them back and ask students to write a few paragraphs using only their notes. The two-week delay forces them to rely on their notes, rather than on their memory of the article.

Presenting Our Findings

Teachers usually assign reports on research findings, but I want to give my students a choice about how they will demonstrate their knowledge. Before they select a specific research area, we talk about how they will present their information, since this can affect their topic selection. Nick decided to research the life of Meriwether Lewis when Stephen, a close friend, suggested they collaborate on a Lewis and Clark role-playing speech for the prairie unit.

My colleagues and I suggest how to present findings, but often the students have better ideas. For example, Kristi Roberts told me her class liked the idea of researching insects that live in the land biomes but didn't like pairing insect pictures with key facts on the bulletin board. Instead, they suggested representing the insects in many ways—three-dimensional bugs hanging from the ceiling, clay bugs in jars, or pop-out bugs on the bulletin board—in addition to writing a summary. Kristi agreed to let her students represent their findings as they suggested, an affirmation of her students.

I compare their experience with that of my grandson, Daniel. He was asked to create a mobile to represent the mammals he was researching. The size of the figures on the mobile had to be three inches, no deviations. Not surprisingly, he didn't have much enthusiasm for the task. By giving students opportunities to use individual talents to carry out activities, especially when the activity is related to the chosen topic, students retain some control over their learning. According to Diane Allen and Mary Piersma (1995), "Such a personal investment gives students that inner motivation that all teachers strive to encourage and a positive attitude toward learning" (151).

When they have worked in groups, my students usually create skits to present research information. I give them rehearsal time, often arranging for the

Figure 7–1. Maggie and friends use magic to show what they know about rain forest animals

group presenting that day to eat lunch in the classroom for extra rehearsal time, and they design their costumes and props.

For their project, Maggie, Jessie, John, and Tialiegh presented a magic show on rainforest animals. Maggie, "the magician," stood on a stool holding her magic wand and introducing the rainforest biome. She told the audience that each rainforest animal would tell them about itself when she tapped it with her magic wand. She began with John, the red-eyed frog (see Figure 7–1).

But the most successful way of presenting information in my experience is simulation or role playing. When we studied the five biomes (tundra, rainforest, woodlands, desert, and prairie), I told students to prepare themselves to spend a full day and night (condensed into three hours) in a biome of their choice. I divided the students into five groups and gave them a week to get ready. Each group of five students planned menus, sleeping gear, activities, and clothing according to the "climate." We decided to write in journals during the event to share at the conclusion. Here is a sample plan devised by one group:

Desert Biome

A.M.	Put up tent
	Fix breakfast outside tent
	Clean up
	Go on "hike" (taking water bottles, sunglasses, snacks, cameras, binoculars)
Noon	Fix lunch
P.M.	Take nap—due to desert heat
	Read
	Sketch plants of desert
	Write in Journals
	Fix supper
	Sit around "campfire"
	Play board games
Night	Go to bed
A.M.	Get up
	Fix breakfast
	Write in journals
	Take down tent
	Pack up

On the appointed day they came to school carrying sleeping bags, tents, food, and tools. They were dressed in shorts for the desert and snow gear for the tundra. I had arranged to use a very large room, which I marked off into five territories. We turned the lights off and pulled the shades down to simulate night. They followed their agendas with enthusiasm. Our activities caught the attention of other students in the school, and my students told them why they were pretending to live in the desert, the tundra, and the other biomes and what they did in their biomes. I suspect that students will remember that biome study for years.

A typical fourth-grade activity, giving speeches to classmates, introduces students to note cards, visual aids, and effective public speaking techniques. During our study of the prairie (our science unit), my students assumed the role of someone who lived on the prairie, currently or in the past, did background research, and spoke as that person:

- Kansas farmer today
- prairie homesteader in 1870

- schoolteacher on prairie in 1870
- governor of North Dakota
- Laura Ingalls Wilder
- guide at Mount Rushmore
- Sitting Bull
- wildlife naturalist
- General George Custer

I portrayed Caleb in *Sarah, Plain and Tall* (MacLachlan 1985), a book we read for literature discussion groups. I dressed in overalls and wore a straw hat. I talked about what a young boy's life on the prairie was like in 1870. We did our research in class, and when the speeches were ready, we invited parents (see Figure 7–2).

Students can present what they know in many ways. Some topics are more suitable for individual research, others for group presentation. I try to strike a balance between working alone and in teams.

Evaluating Our Work and Ourselves

In *Negotiating the Curriculum: Educating for the 21st Century*, Garth Boomer comments, "Reflection on the quality of what has been achieved is a way both of

Figure 7–2. Stephen and Nick role play Lewis and Clark

consolidating learning and of increasing the likelihood of improved performance next time" (1992, 43).

What happens during the learning process is as important as the learning itself. My students are responsible for evaluating their own progress, identifying their strengths and their weaknesses, in order to focus on areas that need improvement. I might ask them to:

- Tell the person next to you what you learned today.
- Tell us orally what surprised you in your research today.
- Tell the person next to you what you will improve on next time.
- Fill out the form entitled, "How Am I Doing?" (see Figure 7–3).

At the end of each day, we meet together and record what we've learned on a chart.

Here is a sample:

1. We received pen pal letters. Our pals live in Grand Rapids, Michigan.
2. We took notes on bats. We learned they are shy, nocturnal, harmless, and eat mosquitoes.
3. When we have writing class we need to whisper.
4. A polygon is a figure with three or more sides.
5. We sketched our science experiment results. We learned that round spheres of oil float because oil does not dissolve in water.

Because I have to assign letter grades, I use some traditional assessment methods. At the conclusion of a unit I usually give a test based on the information the class should have learned through research and discussion. I cannot write the test until all the students have presented their research, since every class discovers different things. I can't reuse a test because every class begins with a different knowledge base. Each test is unique, giving it an authenticity that allows me some comfort in assigning letter grades. I also include some open-ended questions:

- What specific topic did you individually research?
- Write down four facts you learned about your topic.
- Write down four facts you learned from observing another presentation.

When a group presents a skit, an oral report, or a role-play the audience responds after the performance. We tell the presenters what was good about their performance, including interesting facts we learned, and make a couple of suggestions for improvement.

If students present their information in a written report, I respond in writing

NAME _Emily_   DATE _10-13_

How Am I Doing?

Self-Reflection

1. An interesting fact I learned today was _I learned That tree can save sap from last year in there trunks and branches to make leaves._

2. A book I found helpful today was _Called tree It as alot of infor mation_

3. I'm having trouble _with takeing notes on my research because I have so much information._

4. Next time I'm going to _Try puting notes down for information instead of writing in complete sentences._

5. I use my research time: (circle one)

    (A) wisely on task   (B) I am wasting my time

        (C) a little of both

Figure 7–3. How Am I Doing? self-reflection

using the criteria we have previously agreed would be important. When we studied oceans, several students chose to research various aquatic mammals and fish for their written report. We established the following criteria:

- Use several resources: nonfiction books, encyclopedias, Internet, videos.
- Put research facts in own words.

- Include drawings or photos.
- Use format designed by the class (specifies area of research, such as description, food, care of young, enemies, life span).

I usually attach a narrative assessment of my own to each report.

A Special Note on Science Experiments

Students explore research questions primarily through reading a wide variety of books, getting information from other people, community trips, demonstrations, simulations, and similar language-based activities. There is no place for experimentation. Twice a week, I include the lab approach in our science lesson to give students experience in the scientific method. Students like hands-on science experiments. They benefit from predicting what will happen and trying to figure out why.

Setting up science experiments takes planning and involves some scrambling for materials. I assign partners, thus cutting the equipment needed in half. I ask parents to send in materials. I also pool resources with my colleagues.

I require a lab write-up every time students perform an experiment to provide documentation for their portfolios and for letter grades.

1. Describe the experiment.
2. Predict what will happen.
3. Describe what happened.
4. Tell why it happened.

I tell students that scientists record the results of their investigations using scientific vocabulary.

A good source of science experiments is the Janice Van Cleave series on biology, astronomy, earth science, physics, and chemistry. Each book contains easy experiments designed for children. My students take a book of their choice home and pick out an experiment to demonstrate to the class. I make up a schedule for the year. Each week, two students come prepared with the necessary materials, and describe and demonstrate an experiment for the class. Students like to perform the experiments for their peers, who are eager to watch. It gives the student experience in process skills, which are valuable in developing logical thinking and confidence. I take their photograph during the experiment. Students mount the picture on a piece of notebook paper and write a brief description of the experiment.

Parents enjoy seeing the pictures at conference time.

In *Children Exploring Their World*, Sean Walmsley (1994) says, "Children can become interested in a topic that the teacher has chosen if the topic is inherently motivating, if the teacher is knowledgeable and enthusiastic about it, and if the teacher takes the time to provide the right kinds of initiating activities" (19).

Recently, Julie, Kristi, and I visited a private school in Shaker Heights and became interested in a unit on bridges in Cleveland being studied in a fourth-grade class. We immediately set about planning for the new school year. We talked about how we could make *bridges* our theme, broadening the topic to include the bridges to each other (in relationships), to the local community (a nearby nursing home), and to the greater community (our pen pal letters to Michigan). Kristi suggested a field trip to the various bridges in Cleveland with our sketchbooks. We are already enthusiastic, and we haven't even got the students' reactions yet!

8

Self-Assessment

A constant source of frustration is the conflict between what I believe about evaluating students and what my school district requires me to do. I believe in authentic assessment, but I must assign letter grades and administer standardized tests. The reality of the situation is that the public at large considers these grades and test scores valid indicators of student progress and good teaching. Lucy Calkins and her colleagues (1998), in *A Teacher's Guide to Standardized Reading Tests*, say, "the public believes that standardized tests are necessary because they hold the educators to higher standards" (34). I don't agree, but my power to change opinion is limited.

Therefore, I supplement test scores and grades with powerful evidence from student self-assessment. When students are involved in the assessment and evaluation of their own learning, a more complete picture of their progress is possible. In this chapter I will share some practical information about how I get students involved.

The Realities of Standardized Testing and Letter Grades

The Ohio Proficiency Test, which I am required to administer, is written by a group of educational experts, covers a large range of topics, and is heralded by legislators, the community, and parents as proof of learning or of failure to learn. Test results and comparisons between districts are printed in local newspapers, and the push is "to teach to the test." We spend many hours preparing the students for and administering this test. In Ohio we give a practice proficiency test in October; the actual weeklong test is given in March. Because the test is based on the state-mandated curriculum, many teachers attempt to cram the entire fourth-grade curriculum in before March.

The sad irony here is that these tests aren't necessary. I could tell legislators which students will fail long before the March test, because I know my students and I know their strengths and weaknesses. I feel certain that almost every fourth-grade teacher in every state is able to do the same. Children with reading and writing difficulties have trouble passing every section, and as classroom teachers, we should know who those students are after just a few weeks of observing them in our classrooms. Yet fourth-grade teachers have no choice when it comes to testing, and school systems are only responding as usual when so much is at stake.

I find being required to assign letter grades equally frustrating. I concur with Alfie Kohn, who, when addressing the annual ASCD conference in 1995, said "grades are neither valid nor reliable measures," and I attempt to give them some validity through rubrics and other self-assessment tools.

Parents need to understand the evaluation system teachers use. Because most parents received letter grades when they attended school, they understand that grading system. Unless I am prepared to explain my assessment practices in detail and to document their children's growth, parents will put too much stake in the familiar and comfortable. And unless administrators support me in using alternative ways of assessing students, I am forced to use grades alone as the only measure.

I Believe in Student Self-Assessment

Elizabeth Schmar (1995), who wrote the chapter "Student Self-Assessment" in *Report Card on Report Cards*, says, "Our goal as educators is to help students become self-evaluators, not only in the school work, but in their everyday life" (183). I agree. My students constantly reflect on what they have learned, orally and in writing. I provide time and various ways for them to respond.

In *A Stone in My Shoe: Teaching Literacy in Times of Change* Lorri Neilsen (1994) points out that "Schools are beginning to look at assessment not as a separate activity from teaching and learning, but as part of the landscape" (120). I find it hard to determine where teaching ends and assessment begins. When the students evaluate their reading discussion groups and talk about the strengths and weaknesses of the discussion, they think about their contribution to the group. They learn to take responsibility for their behavior. Students who do this become lifelong learners. They make decisions about their learning, they assess their growth, and they talk confidently about their learning. Student-led parent conferences are a vehicle for displaying these skills. The cumulative results of daily self-assessment convey more about academic growth than letter grades can.

Reporting to Parents Using Student-Led Conferences

In *Evaluating Literacy*, Robert Anthony and his colleagues (1991) comment, "Wherever practical students should be included and actively involved in the process of evaluating their own progress and sharing their perceptions of their progress with their teachers and parents" (161). A student-led conference is a triangular progress meeting that brings parent, teacher, and student together. Using a portfolio of work selected by the student and the teacher, the student reviews her academic growth in all subject areas and shares and explains that work to her parents. Included with the selections are completed self-assessment forms, rubrics, test results, benchmarks, and written goals (for self-assessment forms and rubrics, see pages 63, 80, 81, 96–97, 109, and 117).

I sometimes ask students why they think I require student-led conferences. A few have some previous experience with them:

HANNAH: So we think about how we are doing.
MOLLIE: Parents can see how much you've learned.
MARY: Parents see if you understand the subject by your telling them about it.
MATT: Parents get the exact idea of how you're doing and not just what the teacher thinks. Teachers and kids often have different ideas about what a kid knows.
BETSY: Leading a conference practices leadership skills.

Good reasons!

Preparation for the Conference

Preparing for a student-led conference is as important as the conference itself. The mental skills I try to nurture include organizing, reflecting, clarifying and summarizing, analyzing, and drawing conclusions. Here are several ways I ensure that students are adequately prepared.

Creating a time line: For conferences in the second week of March, I begin in January by making out a time line for myself. The time line is a dated list of student assignments that will form their portfolios. Without this schedule, the students and I would be scrambling at the last minute. A time line might look like this:

January 20
Revise conference agenda with the students: "What will happen during the conference?"

January 26–30

1. Business letter for writing folder
2. Science experiment write-up
3. Reading benchmark: "Papa's Parrot" *Every Living Thing* by Cynthia Rylant

February 2–6

1. Self-evaluation of independent self-selected reading (WEB)
2. Sample of friendly letter (Pen Pal letter)
3. Health quiz
4. Math test

February 9–12

1. Math quiz on math facts
2. Review writing notebook for organizational purposes
3. Reading self-evaluation
4. Mapping skills booklet on Ohio

February 17–20

1. Math quiz on math facts
2. Self-evaluation of work habits
3. Random spelling sample as spelling benchmark (dictation)
4. Spelling self-evaluation
5. Health quiz

February 23–27

1. Test on state of Ohio unit
2. Problem-solving sample from math spiral
3. Math quiz on facts
4. Written comparison of present writing with early fall sample
5. Science experiment write-up
6. Video of student-led conference from last year

March 2–6

1. Students organize portfolios according to agenda
2. Students take notes on agenda, watching model of how to do student-led conference
3. I check each portfolio
4. Math test on division
5. I check WEB logs (list of independent reading)
6. Students practice student-led conferences with kindergarten pals and peers

March 9–13

1.   Revisit previous goals and write tentative new ones (Monday)
2.   Student-led conferences (Tuesday, Thursday, Friday)

Writing up the conference agenda: The agenda is an essential tool because it gives students a plan to follow.

Using the assignments from this time line organized by subject, I map out a tentative agenda leading up to the conference. The agenda provides them with the security of knowing what pieces to show their parents.

We revise my agenda together. The end product may look like this:

Reading

1.   Reading logs for Nov–Feb (the trimester)
2.   Reading rubric
3.   WEB evaluation: "Thinking About Your Reading" (see Figure 8–1)
4.   Reading Benchmark: "Papa's Parrot"
5.   Written questions from literature book (in spiral)

Writing

1.   Writing Notebook
2.   Sample of present writing
3.   Writing from fall and present for comparison
4.   Writing rubric

Spelling

1.   Grammar Test
2.   Spelling benchmark

Social Studies / Science

1.   Mapping booklet
2.   Test on Ohio unit
3.   Science experiment write-ups (2)
4.   Photo of science experiment demonstration with written description

Health

1.   Quizzes
2.   Worksheets (KWL on Blood / Teeth)

Math

1.   Rubric—What we've covered from December to March
2.   Problem of the Day sample in Math spiral
3.   Math Quizzes on facts (3)
4.   Math Tests (fractions, averaging, problem solving, division)

Thinking About Your Reading

Date __2-24__   Name __Nick__

1. How often did you read?

   ☐ everyday ☑ most days ☐ not often

2. Check the different kinds (genres) of books that you read.

✓	Fiction	___	Poetry
___	Biography	✓	Mystery
✓	Non-fiction	___	Science-fiction
✓	Historical-fiction	___	Picture books

3. When you look at your log/record, what do you notice about the kinds (levels) of books you are reading? Are most of them:

   ☐ easy (familiar or you knew all the words)
   ☑ medium (just right)
   ☐ hard (needed some help or difficult to understand)

4. What was your favorite book to read? Tell why.

   Mossflower because it has a lot of action. There are lots of tricks and It is not solved quickly.

5. What would you like to read next?

   The next book in the *Redwall* series. (I don't know what it is.)

Figure 8–1. Thinking About Your Reading form

Work Habits
1. Self-evaluation of habits

Goals
1. Review previous goals: Did I succeed?
2. Set new goals

Hannah remarked, "I liked the way everything was based on the agenda."

Organizing the portfolio of work: I use the term "portfolio" to refer to the pocket folder containing selections of student work and self-assessment forms. These folders are stored in a large basket to be easily accessible. I remind students to select work samples periodically from all academic subjects to file in their folder. Nick thought his science experiment write-up on batteries and bulbs was a good example of a weekly experiment, so he put it in his portfolio folder. I may add pieces of work I want parents to see or students to use in documenting their growth from fall to spring. During the first week in March we organize our portfolios according to the agenda so that all items listed on the agenda are in the portfolio (except the oversize writing notebook).

Anyone entering our classroom during the afternoon would see students spread out all over the room, rifling through their papers, which they clip together by subject with large paper clips, referring to their agendas, and calling out, "Mrs. Servis,"

"I can't find my science write-up for mystery powders."
"Where is my Ohio Test?"
"Did you pass back the WEB evaluation?"
"I'm missing my photo of my science experiment."

Everyone is energized by the importance of the event.

I check every portfolio, but I rarely complete the inspection during class, and look through the remaining portfolios after school. When a student passes inspection (when all pieces are in order according to the agenda), I ask him to help someone else. These who finish first are better organized, and able to lend a hand to others having difficulty.

Preparing parents: It is important that parents understand why I hand the leadership of the conference over to the student. I send home a letter informing parents about the conference and explaining its purpose.

Dear Families,

We are busy preparing for the student-led conferences and I want to share some thoughts with you concerning the conferences.

This extended conference time should provide a wonderful learning opportunity for all of us: student, parents, and teachers. As parents you will have the opportunity to express a positive interest in your child's learning, to accept her/his self-evaluations of accomplishments, and give encouragement and support. During the conference we will revisit goals and set new ones for the next trimester.

Some of the goals the students hope to accomplish by leading the conferences are:

- learning to communicate clearly about his/her learning and growth
- learning organizational and leadership skills
- building confidence and self-esteem

The length of the conferences is forty-five minutes. It is essential that you arrive promptly and that we conclude on time.

Please indicate first, second, and third choice of a conference time.

The students and I are looking forward to being with you during this learning celebration.

Sincerely,
Joan Servis

Sample Questions or Comments for Parents to Use during the Conference

~ **Make positive comments.**
"I'm really proud of the work that you have shown us."
"I can see that you are getting better at..."
"I can see that you tried very hard."
"I'm so impressed with the way you conducted your conference."

~ **Ask specific questions about your child's work/learning.**
"Why did you choose to share this particular piece of work?"
"What learning does this work show?"
"What will you learn next?"

~ **Give positive feedback**
"I can really see the growth in your..."
"I'm amazed that you know how to..."
"I didn't know you could..."

~ **Express confidence in your child's ability to lead the conference**
"I can see that you are really organized and ready to begin your conference."
"You are doing a great job conducting this conference."
"I can hardly wait until your next conference."
"I know that you are very talented. Today I have seen many examples of your talents."

~ **Help your child to formulate goals**
"Now that we have seen your work, what do you think you should work on next?"
"What steps will you need to follow to reach your goal?"
"Are these goals possible? Is your time line reasonable?"
"What can I do to help you reach your goals?"
"How will you know when you have reached your goal?"

Figure 8–2. Sample questions or comments for parents to use during the conference

Two weeks before the conferences I send parents sample questions or comments from *Student-Led Conferences* by Janet Millar Grant, Barbara Heffler, and Kadri Mereweather, who point out that "Attendance [at conferences] miraculously improves when students 'perform.' When the conference is really important to the children, they will make sure that their parents attend" (1995, 44). They do (see Figure 8–2).

Rehearsing: The first year I tried student-led conferences, students didn't rehearse, and that was a mistake. They lacked confidence and pacing. To help them feel more comfortable with the process, I model a student-led conference for the class. I selected Betsy to play the student because she was organized and had excellent diction and stage presence. At lunch over a period of about three days, I met with her and Michelle Raeder, the student teacher, who pretended to be Betsy's mother. We rehearsed appropriate comments, for Betsy:

- This is a sample of the type of questions I write for reading discussion.
- That concludes the section on reading. Do you have any questions?
- This math rubric shows you the math strands we've covered during this trimester.
- Now Mrs. Servis will talk about goal setting.

and for her mother (Michelle):

- I can see you understand what you read.
- I didn't know you had memorized your math facts.
- What will you work on next?
- I am so impressed with the way you conducted your conference.

Five minutes on each agenda item plus ten minutes at the end for goal setting added up to a total conference time of forty-five minutes. Betsy practiced within that time frame. When Betsy and Michelle were ready, they demonstrated the student-led conference for the class, while I videotaped it (if I hadn't had a student teacher, I would have played the role of parent). Referring to their agendas, the students watched and took notes on Betsy's comments to help them remember what to say at their own conference (see Figures 8–3a and 8–3b).

When all the students were ready to practice, I grouped them in pairs. On two consecutive afternoons they rehearsed, getting feedback from their partner. In order to cover the entire agenda, I gave the students two more afternoons to practice with a different partner. To help them spend five minutes on each subject, I rang a bell to tell them when to move on to the next academic subject. Gradually the students came to rely on the clock. Students who

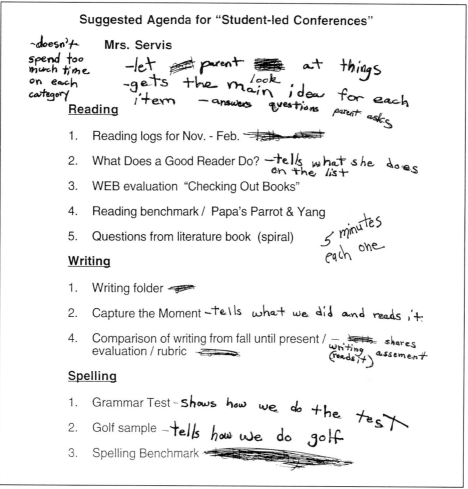

Figure 8–3a. Student's notes on agenda

needed extra help received it during lunch or whenever I could assist them one-on-one.

The Conference

Conference day is a special day. I put out cookies and punch. The students carefully select what they will wear. Usually both parents of each child attend. The students cover their agenda, brimming with confidence and requiring minimum prompting from me because of all the preparation we did. Sometimes I have to remind them to move on to the next item to stay on schedule (see Figure 8–4).

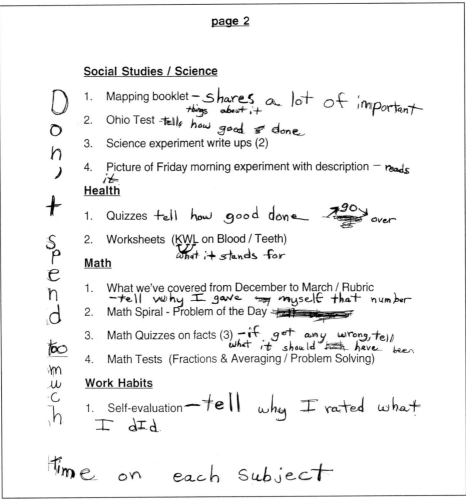

Figure 8–3b. Student's notes on agenda

JENNY: I'd like to tell you how I am doing in writing. Here's my Writing Notebook. I have my rough drafts and revisions in here. For example, here are my rough drafts for the story I wrote about a girl at camp [*shows parent section in notebook labeled fiction*].

DAD: I can see you made lots of changes in the story.

JENNY: I read my piece to someone and they give me suggestions.

MOM: How do you get the ideas?

JENNY: I get ideas from other students.

DAD: Do you take the suggestions?

Figure 8–4. Jenny shares her progress with her parents during a student-led conference

JENNY: Most of them. It makes my writing better. Here's an example of how I've improved in writing. Here's a piece I wrote the first week of school and I'm going to compare it to an article I wrote for the newsletter last week [*reads the short selections aloud*]. In the fall I did not use a good lead. I now use catchy leads. I used to use overworked words like nice and good. Now I use more descriptive vocabulary. I didn't always use correct spelling in the fall—see all the mistakes? Now I am much better.

MOM: I can see you have improved a lot.

JENNY: I only wrote poetry in the fall. Now I like to write fiction and articles for our newsletter.

MRS. SERVIS: Jenny, we need to move to the writing rubric.

JENNY: Okay. Here's a writing rubric which describes what a good writer does. I'm going to show you what I'm working on to improve.

During the last ten minutes we set manageable goals for the next trimester. We use the draft of tentative goals and the action-plan students brainstormed during class. Students usually have a clear understanding of what they need to improve, although parent and teacher suggestions may prompt them to revise goals (see Figure 8–5).

Most conferences go smoothly, but there are usually one or two that are difficult. Susan, tense and nervous, burst into tears and was unable to complete her

MARCH

Goal:

1. I need to study a little bit more for tests so I have more confidence in myself.

2. I am going to write in more various genres.

3. I need to check and see if I have everything I'm supposed to before I leave.

Action Plan:

1. I'm going to take all the papers home that I am supposed to and study about 10 minutes each night before a test.

2. I am going to write short stories in different genres.

Signatures: *Eli Dilner-Dunlap*

Figure 8–5. Goals with action plan

conference. Later, her mother and I talked privately, and she recognized the pressure she was putting on her child to achieve perfection. Similarly, Dave was unable to lead his conference without lots of prompting because he was missing many samples of his work. I had been reporting this problem to the parents, but it became clear during the conference. Difficult conferences, though never enjoyable, often give parents a clearer picture of their child's situation.

Feedback

I invite parents and students to let me know their reactions to what is sometimes their first experience with student-led conferences.

Hilary Colvin, Maggie's mother, wrote, "Student-led conferences (in the higher grade levels) are so valuable because not only do you get a sense of how your child is doing, you know your child has a clear understanding of their strengths and their weaknesses. Their goals are important to them because they've helped formulate them and discussing them as a group keeps us all on the same page."

Dr. Bernard Silver, Mollie's father, wrote, "This was a great exercise for her, allowing her to present her own work to parents and teachers and receive immediate feedback—a great confidence builder."

Bakari's mother, Crystal Lewis, summarized her thoughts about her first student-led conference, "To me it seemed that the student-led conference gave the student an opportunity to get an overall view of fourth grade. It gave him a chance to objectively look at himself and his learning. I think this is a valuable skill; to be able to look objectively at a situation that we are in. This may help in other areas of life. I also think it made the student feel empowered *and* responsible for his own results and effort. Being responsible for ourselves and accepting the consequences of our behavior (positive and negative) is another skill that is transferable to various life situations.

I can see how a student-led conference could also be a valuable feedback for a teacher. A teacher could see, too, how effective her objectives and teaching style were reaching the student."

Eli's mother, Amy Dibner said, "I liked being witness to the interaction between Eli and his teachers. There's a level of respect and comfort that I enjoyed seeing."

When I ask students about how they felt, they say,

- I felt like I was a teacher.
- It was hard because I've never talked to my parents about my education before.
- Before the conference I was nervous but felt relaxed after I got started.
- It was a great experience. It makes me feel responsible.
- I like knowing what I need to do.
- I learned how to explain stuff.
- Instead of asking the teacher what I'm not doing, she would have to ask me.
- I liked that I got to do the talking so my parents could see what I think.
- I liked that the focus was on me and not the teacher.
- I liked how I was the leader and I got to explain everything.
- I felt like I was a grown-up and not a fourth grader.
- I liked how I felt like I was running the show.

I agree wholeheartedly with David, who said, "It was lots of work and took a long time to get ready, but it's worth it." Positive feedback motivates me to make that extra effort even though fitting all the conferences into my schedule is a major investment of time. And it is reassuring to hear how independent the students felt.

Alternatives to Student-Led Conferences

If you cannot carve out the time for student-led conferences, there are less demanding alternatives that also involve students and have been positively received by parents.

Triangular Teacher-Led Conferences

When the student, parent, and teacher are present, the teacher can lead the conference. Parents do not have to repeat what the teacher said when they get home and sometimes problems can be cleared up on the spot. "John, tell us about these assignments you did not complete." At the end of the conference, which can be completed in twenty minutes, the three parties together can set goals for the student.

Parents have responded favorably. For example, Matt's mother, Sondra Saddler, told me that when a child hears what he needs to do from a teacher with a parent present, it makes a greater impact. She also feels that the child needs to be part of the conference to emphasize communication between home and school.

Kirsten's mother, Cathy Whitehouse, asked, "How can a child be accountable for learning unless she is an integral part of the process?" The best part of having her daughter present, she said, was witnessing the dialogue between Kirsten and her teacher. It was reassuring to see how comfortable her daughter was with the teacher.

Stations

Several teachers in my district use performance stations as an alternative to student-led conferences. The teacher sets up five stations: math, writing, social studies and science, reading, and goal setting. At each station a child shows his parents what he has learned about the subject with the help of his folder and the manipulatives at the station. The teacher meets them at the goal-setting station, where they review the tentative goals. The only drawback of this alternative is that parents wish the teacher could be present at each station to field questions.

According to Lisa Bietau (1995), "Collaborative conferencing has benefits for all stakeholders. However, students especially have the opportunity to practice an essential life skill. When collaboration is practiced in a meaningful context, and dedicated to enhanced student progress, it is well worth the time, effort, and energy required" (153). A new administrator asked me, "Why do you want to do all that work having student-led conferences? It's not required." My answer: "It's worth it!" The process encourages independence, links daily self-assessment to goal setting and reporting to parents, and completes the evaluation picture in a way that letter grades or standardized tests alone cannot.

9

Together We Can . . .

There was a time in my career when I closed my classroom door and worked in isolation with my students and my teacher's manual. To make matters worse, I felt I had to pretend that I knew what I was doing. I remember once being called to the principal's office and asked, "What is your weak area?" Since I didn't want the principal to think I didn't know exactly what I was doing all the time, I replied, "I do not have a weak area. I'm good at everything." My rationale was, "I'm not giving away anything. If the principal thinks I'm weak in some area, let her notice it and bring it to my attention."

Today, not only do I admit my weaknesses but I look to my colleagues for help. We learn from each other. In almost every classroom in our building visitors will see a bulletin board labeled "Message Board" used by both teachers and students for personal notes, announcements, jokes, lists, clippings on current events, sign-up sheets, and letters to the entire class. Most of the staff does not know that the idea comes from Jerome C. Harste, Kathy G. Short, and Carolyn Burke's *Creating Classrooms for Authors: The Reading-Writing Connection.* The teachers in my building have learned it from each other; they see it observing it in other classrooms, and ask how it works. What a change. My colleagues and I communicate and collaborate.

Grade-Level Teams

The fourth-grade teachers meet as a team each month to plan field trips, write group letters to parents about conferences, and organize other events. When we plan our units of study, we spread out the workload. We share strategies as well as books, videos, and other materials for teaching particular units.

Being a member of the fourth-grade team isn't without its bumps. I find myself having to compromise, sometimes doing more than my share, and being patient with a noncontributing colleague. Yet I would still recommend it enthusiastically as a way not simply of heading off complaints from parents but of lightening each individual's responsibilities.

Parents also feel happier when all fourth-grade classrooms operate in a similar manner—taking the same field trips, for example, and handling reporting uniformly. We make sure that all students are offered the same experiences, and we split up the tasks. Every year each team member organizes a field trip, for instance, taking full responsibility for ordering buses, arranging for chaperones, handling fees, and confirming the dates on the calendar.

I never want to return to the days when I went to the library to get books for teaching a content area only to discover that another fourth-grade teacher had them all. I would have to ask the teacher when she would finish teaching the unit and switch my own schedule around. What a joy it is to share the materials and collaborate on ways to enrich the curriculum! And we draw on the collective expertise of four teachers in planning the units.

Our former principal, Rosemary Weltman, always sympathetic to heavy teaching demands, provided our team with "release time" to meet with Marianne Bursi, the enrichment teacher. The enrichment program at Onaway, once designed only for the "gifted" students, now provides challenging lessons for all of our students. Marianne worked with our students to dig more deeply into a topic, using innovative and stimulating approaches tailored to each student.

In November, for example, we planned a unit on the rainforest biome as part of our science curriculum. Marianne had visited the rainforest and brought back slides, artifacts, and souvenirs. We decided to introduce the unit by asking Marianne to show her slides to the class and talk about her trip. She could spend one morning or afternoon a week with each of our classes. We divided our individual classes into two groups, each group working about five weeks with Marianne and five weeks with the classroom teacher, and then switching. In this way, each teacher could work with only twelve students at a time. This plan was so successful it has been incorporated throughout the district.

At another meeting, as our team lamented about not having enough time to plan our student-led conferences, we decided to draft a letter to our principal. In our letter we emphasized the need for collaboration time during school because we lacked creative energy at the end of a teaching day. Rosemary Weltman granted our request. Our strong team position, presented clearly in writing, had an impact on her decision. I often tell my students that two or more brains working together are better than one. I encourage teachers to pool their resources and talents to enjoy the benefits of group collaboration.

Teacher Support Group

One of the best vehicles for sharing our struggles and our successes is the weekly Teacher Support Group meeting, which is voluntary, open to teachers at all grade levels—and well attended. We determine our agenda according to the interests of the group, and it appears in the weekly bulletin given to every staff member on Fridays. In the fall, we talk about topics we'd like to cover and narrow them down by a show-of-hands vote. Sometimes new district policies dictate our needs: for example, implementing retelling as a comprehension strategy will soon be required of all teachers of primary grades. We discuss what role phonics plays in reading, what student work to put in portfolios, which spelling words we expect children to know in each grade, and other current topics. We read and discuss professional books as well as articles from educational journals. When we wanted more information about student-led conferences, for example, we turned to *Student-Led Conferences* by Janet Millar Grant, Barbara Heffler, and Kadri Mereweather.

Teachers who attend off-site workshops bring new ideas back to the group, and we pass along information on upcoming workshops and conferences.

Last November, one of our meetings focused on whether student work posted on hall bulletin boards must be spelled correctly. It was almost time for our first parent conferences, and the new teachers wanted to know how we had handled this problem in the past. After a stimulating discussion about displaying young children's invented spellings, we agreed that most papers must have either correct spelling or some indication that the teacher permitted invented spelling (several teachers offered to share their "unedited" stamps). Since one of the misconceptions of the whole language approach is that spelling is not important, the new teachers wanted parents to realize that they cared as much about spelling as about content. We agreed that the average person does not "see" past a spelling error and wanted to make certain parents could not level that criticism at any teacher in Onaway School.

Sometimes our meetings include demonstrations. We asked Regie Routman to demonstrate teaching strategies for fourth graders who are having reading problems. We also agreed that we wanted to observe how to teach fiction writing and literature groups, focusing on the kinds of questions that would inspire good discussions. We have discovered the value of encouraging one another.

Teammates

I can't imagine teaching without Julie Beers, my fourth-grade colleague. When Regie Routman (1996) writes that daily interaction with her colleagues "keeps teaching intellectually exciting and rewarding for me" (173), I think of how well that phrase fits our relationship. Julie and I are in and out of each other's classrooms constantly, sharing books and materials. We change our teaching if something worked well—or didn't—in the other's class. The best part is that our students see and hear us assisting each other, which is precisely what we want them to do.

Julie and I share a common philosophy about how to work with children. We think alike and approach things from a similar point of view. We question what we do in the classroom: "Is this what *I* do as a reader or a writer? Is this necessary? Is it the best way to learn?" We think carefully about our procedures and about our study units.

Although Julie happens to be over thirty years younger and previously taught third grade, I have discovered that these differences don't matter. What does matter is that we are excited about what we are doing and enjoy bouncing ideas off one another.

Julie and I exchange our notes from conferences and workshops. Last year, the day I returned to school after the International Reading Association Conference, Julie and I met for lunch. Bubbling over with enthusiasm, I told her about various seminars I had attended and speakers I had heard.

Together, we decided to purchase sketch pads for drawing, observing, writing, and reflecting as a result of a presentation by Karen Ernst (1997). As she demonstrates in *Picturing Learning: Artists and Writers in the Classroom*, Karen, a former art teacher, believes in connecting reading and writing with art. She has successfully integrated a writing workshop approach with an elementary art curriculum. Julie and I realized that some of our students are talented artists and would have more opportunity to excel in an area we were neglecting if we adopted her ideas.

During one of our summer planning sessions, Julie and I considered how we might use sketch pads. We thought about using them for responding to poetry, for sketching landscapes, for copying famous art masterpieces, and for science observations (drawings of the science experiment would illustrate the student's write-up). We decided to ask the students for their ideas when school began. One idea suggested was to ask parents to sketch in the books during Open House. The entire class enjoyed seeing the sketches drawn by parents.

In the fall, Julie said to me, "Are you sketching when your students do? Did you give yourself a sketch pad?" "No, but I'm changing that today," I replied, and immediately bought myself a sketch pad and started sketching. It's easy to forget the importance of leading by joining in.

Although summer sessions enable us to make long-range plans and give us new ideas, we address some topics throughout the school year:

- Spelling: We're never satisfied with our program. This past year we purchased lots of spelling games to give students an opportunity to play with words. This has proved popular with students, and it has even improved their spelling.
- Homework: Julie suggested that students survey family members and friends about their favorite flavor of ice cream and record the data on a graph. In class we would model the assignment by giving the students dishes of ice cream—vanilla, strawberry, or chocolate—and illustrate their choices on a graph.
- Science Theme Study: We tried new ways of teaching about the biomes, designing lessons as we went. Glynae, a student from my class, shared her biome research with Julie's class, and told them how she took notes and wrote up a minireport. She served as a model for Julie's students as they approached the same task.
- Writing: My class was having difficulty thinking of topics to write about in writing class. Julie sent over several students to tell us how they got ideas for their writing. Doug said he went to a local book store and browsed, getting ideas for topics by scanning book jackets.

Collaborating has become a habit. Our strengths are combined, our skills refined, and our mutual enthusiasm shared. I urge teachers to forge a partnership with someone who shares a common philosophy about teaching.

Mentoring

Entry-year teachers in Shaker Heights schools are assigned a mentor at their grade level. The role of the mentor is to help the new teacher adjust to the demanding job of teaching. The mentor receives a stipend and must attend several formal programs with the new teacher. In August for example, there is a two-day workshop for getting acquainted and mapping out the curriculum and our goals for the year. The district provides release time for classroom observation.

Within the past ten years I have mentored six teachers new to my district, and have found the experience both gratifying to me and helpful to the new teacher. The new teacher benefits by having someone guiding her through an unfamiliar curriculum, providing procedures for implementing every subject, giving her materials, and assisting her in establishing routines. The mentor benefits because the new teacher asks questions and brings a fresh perspective to a familiar landscape:

- How do you help students pace themselves in completing a project?
- What do you do to encourage students to revise their written pieces?

- Why don't you give timed tests for math facts?
- What about the student who makes lots of spelling errors? Do you require that student to correct all mistakes?
- Why don't you give a weekly spelling test?

Once, when I was explaining my system of checks, check pluses, and check minuses on homework to a new teacher—the check meant the work was okay, the check plus that it was exceptional, and the check minus that it needed improvement—she asked, "Why are you using check and check plus? Isn't it either okay or not okay?"

I thought about it for a few days and realized I could eliminate check plus. An assignment was either satisfactory or it needed further work.

Before Shaker Heights instituted a formal mentoring program, there was an informal one. The principal asked veteran teachers to assist new teachers. Many schools do this. I always welcomed the opportunity because the enthusiasm and commitment new teachers bring to the job is contagious. They recharge and reinvigorate my teaching. Usually new teachers, overwhelmed and barely keeping their heads above water, are grateful for help. And I feel good sharing my experience. Isn't that what I ask my students to do? Too often, veteran teachers expect new ones to "pay their dues"—no supplies, no ideas, no collegiality. I recall that when I started out as a new teacher, my classroom (like Mother Hubbard's cupboard) was bare, raided by veteran teachers before I arrived, a not uncommon practice even today.

Yet I am encouraged, and I agree wholeheartedly with Lucy Calkins (1991) when she says, "Teachers are coming together. We're coming together across districts, across grade levels and disciplines, even within our own staff rooms, and we're coming together in the spirit of an old-fashioned barn raising. It's not a barn we're building but a better world for ourselves and our children" (304).

Cross-Grade Collaborations

For several years, Susan Mears and I have been bringing her kindergarten class and my fourth-grade class together for activities. We like to think the fourth graders can be models for the kindergartners, especially in reading and writing. We randomly pair up the younger and older students for the year, and they meet every week for about thirty minutes. Fourth graders enter the kindergarten room carrying picture books they like and have selected for reading to their pals. The kindergartners, gathered on the rug, are often in the midst of a song, usually one familiar to the fourth graders, since many of them had Mrs. Mears for a teacher. Smiling, the fourth graders sit on the rug with their pals to join in. At the conclusion of the song, half of the partners remain in Susan's class and the other half return to mine, holding each others' hands as they go up the big stairs. We rotate the room assignments periodically.

When the children finish reading their books together or writing stories, we allow them to decide what they want to do next. They may choose to work on the computer, play games, play with the pets, color, draw, or build with blocks. Fourth graders adore being back in the kindergarten classroom, with all the colorful objects to touch, and kindergartners feel grown up exploring the big fourth-grade classroom.

Susan and I designed a yearlong schedule of thematic monthly events for these cross-grade collaborations. In January we planned a birthday party for Martin Luther King, Jr. Students would perform a play and then enjoy refreshments with their pals and invited guests.

When Shelley Harwayne, the principal of the Manhattan New School in New York City, visited Shaker Heights for a workshop, I invited her for dinner and proudly showed her the plan Susan and I had designed. She looked it over and said, "Are the children going to have the opportunity to revise this plan?" I hadn't given a thought to asking the students what they would like to do. I had been so pleased with the outline, I had left out the group that would have to follow it! In *Negotiating the Curriculum* Nancy Lester says, "What stands out for me is the continuing conflict I see . . . in our actions and in our reflections . . . between transmitting and constructively negotiating" (151). It's so true. I had embraced reflection but overlooked negotiation.

Following Shelley's advice I took the plan to my fourth graders and asked for their ideas. Some activities stayed and some were eliminated, and new ideas were added. We spent a long writing period discussing and agreeing on the changes. In the end, Susan and I had not wasted our time, because it was helpful to have a framework to revise.

The following year, to save time, we used the revised plan, but the new classes did not respond well. Susan and I realized that we need to involve our students in the planning every year; otherwise, the activities are something done to students, not something they want to do. Sometimes I wonder if I will ever learn.

For the third year of our collaboration, we gave fourth graders and kindergartners time to go over the plan together. We told them to keep in mind the overall purpose of literary pals and to think about new suggestions for reading and writing. They came up with lots of new ideas (see Figure 9–1).

In the end, we made several changes. In October we would have ghost stories and a Halloween party. In November we would make turkeys together out of apples and marshmallows, and have pizza. The classes love the Martin Luther King, Jr., birthday party with a Reader's Theater and overwhelmingly voted to keep it on the list of January activities. Susan typed up the revised plan:

Figure 9–1. Shelly, a fourth grader, discusses reading and writing with her kindergarten pal

Pal Plans (Revised)

October Activities

Ghost stories—Fourth-grade students will choose ghost stories to read to their pals. Students will explore literacy through ghost stories.

Halloween play—Fourth-grade students will choose a play prior to meeting with pals. The students will rehearse the play that will be performed at the next session. The students will discuss the Halloween party and assign jobs. Students will explore literacy through a play and making lists.

Halloween party—Presentation of play and refreshments.

November Activities

Pizza Day together—Students will have pizza together in the multipurpose room and share each other's company. Fourth-grade students will read stories afterwards.

Turkey project—Students will make turkeys together. Students will have to investigate various ideas for turkeys (in craft books), choose an idea, gather the materials, and work cooperatively with their pal to construct the turkey.

December Activities

ABC–1, 2, 3—Students will explore ABC and 1, 2, 3 books and help their pals make a book.

Games in the snow—Students will explore various games that can be played in the snow, gather the materials, and play the games.

January Activities

MLK birthday and Reader's Theater—Students will be divided into groups to work on various committees for a MLK birthday celebration (such as invitations for administrators). Students will share books on MLK for ideas to use in the Reader's Theater.

Students will continue to practice their Reader's Theater assignments for the upcoming celebration. The fourth-grade students will carry out the major part of the performance with the kindergarten students as the chorus throughout the reading. Students will be involved in all aspects of a performance and become familiar with the format of Reader's Theater.

Birthday party for Martin Luther King—Students will perform and then enjoy refreshments with their pals and other spectators. They will gain knowledge of African American history by learning about the life of MLK.

Susan and I now agree that talking and planning with students is more important than the activities we do.

In the spring, students bring their parents to view the classrooms and the displays of their work. Recently, I saw a parent I didn't recognize. As I approached her, I saw that she was with her kindergarten child, who was one of my student's literary pals.

The mother said, "My daughter insisted I come up here to meet her fourth-grade pal, Jessica. She talks about her all the time."

When I relayed this incident to Susan, we began to reflect on what the students gain from the experience. Susan said, "The children benefit from having someone next to them, arm to arm, conversing about the pictures and enjoying the physical intimacy of sharing a book." She compared the fourth graders to grandparents or siblings without "family baggage."

I asked my students what they have learned from working with kindergarten children. Most of their observations were related to helping them read and write:

- CHRIS: I find it is hard to teach. I have trouble getting my pal to write about his picture. He writes about something else.
- HANNAH: I have learned not all kids use the same strategies in learning to read.

- MOLLIE: They don't know vowels.
- STEPHEN: They have trouble reading complicated words.
- ELENA: They get tired sooner.
- BETSY: My pal didn't pay attention when I read a book to her until I started using lots of expression. Now she pays attention.

Several students agreed that they, like Betsy, have had to read aloud with more expression. Working with the kindergartners has given all the fourth graders a sense of accomplishment, made them more sensitive to others, and improved their performance. As the year progressed they became more careful in selecting books, thinking about what their pals would like rather than their own interests.

Susan reported that the kindergartners are deeply disappointed if we miss a session, and many parents have told me how much their child loves having a kindergarten pal. The bonding between the two grades is strong. John wrote the following article for our last issue of our classroom newsletter.

Zachattack

I will never forget Zachary Hopkins. He was the best care pal I ever had. He was always in a happy mood. He was never in a bad mood. He was a very kind and generous kid. I felt like he was my little brother. I will always remember him. He will always have a place in my heart.

Parent Partners

Every fall since 1991 I've been asking parents to write to me about their child. I found the idea in Lucy Calkins' *Living Between the Lines* and use a similar letter to enlist the parents' help in learning about their child's interests and learning style. The first line of my letter begins, "I'm writing to ask you to help me become a partner with you in your child's education." Parents respond with heartfelt observations and descriptions of sons and daughters.

Often the letters begin with, "Thank you for asking us to write about Kristen" or "Thank you for the opportunity to share with you about Eli." One parent included a poem her child dictated to her when he was five years old and told me he's sure to be an author some day. One letter that made me smile stated, "Unfortunately he has picked up some annoying habits from his father, such as an unrelenting need for everything to be exactly right."

Mary Beth Lasky began her letter about her daughter Michaela with, "Five years at Onaway and you are the first teacher to really come out and ask *ME* to describe my child; not that the others didn't want to know but you seem genuinely interested and as a parent it is refreshing." She ended her letter with "Thank you for giving me the opportunity to reflect on my child. It's something I need to do more often."

One parent told me she had written about her child but realized her letter was too negative and never gave it to me.

Jim Rebitzer closed his three-page letter: "As I write this letter I realize I am very proud of Hannah. I think she is growing up to be a warm, caring, interesting and engaging person." Many parents close their letters with "We love our child very much!"

I try to make parents feel welcome early on, at the September curriculum meeting, when I have a captive audience for forty-five minutes. I pass out an open-house packet containing information about each subject, my goals and philosophy, homework expectations, portfolio sharing, and an invitation to visit the classroom. I do not go over the packet at the curriculum meeting, but simply urge the parents to read it. Instead, with the time I have, I help them get to know me. I read poetry, tell funny stories, and in general entertain them. I tell them I'm a grandparent, how disorganized one of my grandsons is, and the advice I give my daughter. I tell them humorous things their children have said. I tell them what I love about fourth graders, what a wonderful class we have, and what excellent manners their children are exhibiting.

I usually end with a poem from *Stories I Ain't Told Nobody Yet* by Jo Carson:

> I am asking you to come back home
> before you lose the chance of seein' me alive.
> You already missed your daddy.
> You missed your uncle Howard.
> You missed Luciel.
> I kept them and I buried them.
> You showed up for the funerals.
> Funerals are the easy part.
>
> You even missed that dog that you left.
> I dug him a hole and put him in it.
> It was a Sunday morning, but dead animals
> don't wait no better than dead people.
>
> My mama used to say she could feel herself
> runnin' short of the breath of life. So can I.
> And I am blessed tired of buryin' things I love.
> Somebody else can do that job to me.
> You'll be back here then; you come for funerals.

I'd rather you come back now and got my stories.
I've got whole lives of stories that belong to you.
I could fill you up with stories,
stories I ain't told anybody yet,
stories with your name, your blood in them.
Ain't nobody gonna hear them if you don't
and you ain't gonna hear them unless you get back home.
When I am dead, it will not matter
how hard you press your ear to the ground.

When I finish, I ask parents to please tell their children stories about their lives. Quite often parents request a copy of the poem. I've even heard from parents who couldn't attend. One said, "Mrs. Servis, I think I should have been at your open house. I hear you were a real hoot!" I believe in laughing and crying together (there are tears when I read the poem). I want the parents to come to the classroom again.

Not only do I urge parents to visit, I enlist them as helpers. Currently I have parents in my writing class. They confer with students, giving feedback and helping with the editing process. One year I had a parent who felt the students' final writing pieces had to be free of all errors. When she found mistakes in her daughter's published piece, I asked her to come into the classroom during writing class and be a "senior editor," proofreading with students before they wrote their final piece. I told her I could not keep up with twenty-five students.

She agreed to come and help during writing class. As she worked with students, helping them edit, she became aware that the process of editing a paper was a learning experience; students struggled with *why* they were making corrections. The big discovery for her was that even when the paper was edited to perfection, the final piece could have overlooked typing or copying errors. She became a supporter of the process instead of a critic. She did a terrific job and I welcomed her help.

Asking parents to share a special talent or area of expertise is another way to include them in our classroom community. I extend invitations at the fall meeting. In newsletters throughout the year, I remind them of the invitation. Often they send notes telling me they are willing, and I follow up with a phone call. Among the parents who have participated,

- Robert Santelli, father of Jenna and author of seven books about music, bicycling, and travel, shared his life as a writer.
- Mary Brownell, mother of Devon Matlock, brought her slides, souvenirs, and food from South America.

- Graphic artist Carol Lombardi, mother of Kevin, shared her portfolio of brochures, posters, booklets, and newsletters she had created and explained how it helped her get a job.
- Dr. Herbert Wiedemann, father of Sarah and a lung specialist, told us about the respiratory system. The fourth-grade health curriculum requires a study of the lungs, so we especially welcomed his willingness to teach us.
- Akila Muhammad, mother of Rasheed, shared the seven principles of Kwanzaa, an African agricultural gathering celebrated by many African American families.

I also give out my home phone number in September and tell parents to please call if they have concerns. Sometimes a message on my answering machine is sufficient. Parents do not abuse the privilege; calls are infrequent and usually helpful to me. I think of parents as partners.

If You Feel Alone

The only reason I presume to give advice to teachers who feel alone and unsupported is that I have been there. I remember what it was like to struggle alone in the classroom. I have some suggestions for teachers:

- Start an evening teacher support group. Pass out flyers to teachers asking them to come to your home to share their ideas about what is working and what isn't. If you have young children or conflicts that prevent evening meetings, invite teachers to join you for lunch. A dessert or refreshments will make it more appealing.
- Seek out a colleague who reads the professional literature. Ask if you can chat about some books or articles. I read constantly and I have discovered many ideas in these sources. Catalogs from Heinemann, the National Council of Teachers of English, Stenhouse, Marilyn Burns Associates, Association for Supervision and Curriculum Development, and the International Reading Association, all published yearly, are excellent sources for selecting books. Check their Web sites, too. Regie Routman's (1994) *The Blue Pages: Resources for Teachers* has comprehensive lists of books, articles, journals, newsletters, and other publications.

  I am aware of the physical demands on teachers and how difficult it is to find the energy to read professionally. Yet if I don't do so regularly, I am not being nourished. I carve out thirty minutes a day, no matter what.
- Seek out the new teacher and provide her with all the help you can give. Develop a friendship, be available, and with luck you can grow together.

- Seek out a teacher on another grade level who shares your philosophy. I collaborated with Julie Beers, a third-grade teacher, for nine years before she switched to fourth grade.
- Invite a teacher you trust into your classroom to observe writing class or reading discussion groups and ask for her reactions.
- Spend your own money to attend workshops if your school system does not have the funds for inservice. Professional development is essential. (Regie Routman has more advice in her book, *Literacy at the Crossroads*).
- Sign up for a student teacher. It gives you another person for collaboration.

Together we can . . .

You don't have to be alone. I encourage you to reach out. When we help one another, recognize the strengths of others, and celebrate one another's successes, students benefit. Teaching does not have to be a lonely job anymore.

References

Allen, Diane D., and Mary L. Piersma. 1995. *Developing Thematic Units: Process and Product*. Albany, NY: Delmar Publishers.

Ames, Louise Bates, and Carol Chase Haber. 1990. *Your Nine-Year-Old: Thoughtful and Mysterious*. New York: Bantam Doubleday Dell Publishing Group, Inc.

Anderson, Jane, and Marceta Reilly. 1995. "Establishing Performance Standards." In *Report Card on Report Cards: Alternatives to Consider*, edited by Tara Azwell and Elizabeth Schmar, 49–58. Portsmouth, NH: Heinemann.

Anthony, Robert J., Terry D. Johnson, Norma L. Mickelson, and Alison Preece. 1991. *Evaluating Literacy: A Perspective for Change*. Portsmouth, NH: Heinemann.

Atwell, Nancie. 1998. *In the Middle: New Understanding About Writing, Reading, and Learning*. Portsmouth, NH: Heinemann.

Avi. 1992. *Who Was That Masked Man, Anyway?* New York: Orchard Books.

Bennett, Albert, and Linda Foreman. 1991. *Visual Mathematics. Vol. 1: Math and the Mind's Eye*. Portland, OR: The Math Learning Center and Portland State University.

Bietau, Lisa. 1995. "Student, Parent, Teacher Collaboration." In *Report Card on Report Cards: Alternatives to Consider*, edited by Tara Azwell and Elizabeth Schmar, 183–95. Portsmouth, NH: Heinemann.

Bolton, Faye, and Diane Snowball. 1993. *Ideas for Spelling*. Portsmouth, NH: Heinemann.

———. 1993. *Teaching Spelling: A Practical Resource*. Portsmouth, NH: Heinemann.

Boomer, Garth, Nancy Lester, Cynthia Onore, and John Cook, eds. 1992. *Negotiating the Curriculum: Education for the 21st Century*. London and Bristol, PA: Falmer.

Brodie, Julie Pier, Rhea Irvine, Cynthia Reah, Ann Roper, Kelly Stewart, and Kathryn Walker. 1996. *Mathland: Journeys Through Mathematics: Daily Tune-Ups 2*. Mountain View, CA: Creative Publications.

Brummett, Micaelia Randolph, and Linda Holden Charles. 1989. *Connections: Linking Manipulatives to Mathematics Grade 4*. Sunnyvale, CA: Creative Publications.

Burns, Marilyn. 1988. *A Collection of Math Lessons from Grades 3 Through 6*. New Rochelle, NY: The Math Solutions Publications.

———. 1992. *About Teaching Mathematics: A K–8 Resource*. White Plains, NY: Cuisenaire.

Calkins, Lucy McCormack, with Shelley Harwayne. 1991. *Living Between the Lines*. Portsmouth, NH: Heinemann.

Calkins, Lucy, Kate Montgomery, Donna Santman, with Beverly Falk. 1998. *A Teacher's Guide to Standardized Reading Tests: Knowledge Is Power*. Portsmouth, NH: Heinemann.

Carson, Jo. 1989. *Stories I Ain't Told Nobody Yet*. New York: Orchard Books.

Clayton, Marlynn K. Winter. 1997. "Teacher Tips: Helpful Ideas for the Responsive Classroom Teacher." *Responsive Classroom* 9 (3): 4–5.

Conly, Jane Leslie. 1986. *Rasco and the Rats of NIMH*. New York: Harper & Row.

Corwin, Rebecca B., with Judith Storeygard, and Sabra L. Price. 1996. *Talking Mathematics: Supporting Children's Voices*. Portsmouth, NH: Heinemann.

Dahl, Roald. 1961. *James and the Giant Peach*. New York: Alfred A. Knopf.

Dewey, Jennifer Owings. 1994. *Wildlife Rescue: The Work of Dr. Kathleen Ramsay*. Honesdale, PA: Boyds Mills Press.

Downie, Diane, Twila Slesnick, and Jean Kerr Stenmark. 1981. *Math for Girls and Other Problem Solvers*. Berkeley, CA: Lawrence Hall of Science, University of California, Math/Science Network.

Dudley-Marling, Curt. 1995. "Complicating Ownership." In *Who Owns Learning: Questions of Autonomy, Choice, and Control*, edited by Curt Dudley-Marling and Dennis Searle, 1–15. Portsmouth, NH: Heinemann.

Eeds, Maryann, and Ralph Peterson. 1990. *Grand Conversations: Literature Groups in Action*. New York: Scholastic.

Ehrlich, Amy, ed. 1996. *When I Was Your Age: Original Stories About Growing Up*. Cambridge, MA: Candlewick Press.

Erlbach, Arlene. 1998. *The Kids' Business Book*. Minneapolis: Lerner Publications.

Ernst, Karen. 1994. *Picturing Learning: Artists and Writers in the Classroom*. Portsmouth, NH: Heinemann.

———. 1997. Connecting Reading, Writing, and Art. Seminar given at annual meeting of International Reading Association, Atlanta, GA, May.

Ferrara, Judith M. 1996. *Peer Mediation: Finding a Way to Care*. York, ME: Stenhouse Publishers.

Fleischman, Paul. 1988. *Joyful Noise: Poems for Two Voices*. New York: Harper & Row.

Florian, Douglas. 1996. *On the Wing: Bird Poems and Paintings*. San Diego: Harcourt Brace & Company.

Fox, Mem. 1993. *Radical Reflections: Passionate Opinions on Teaching, Learning, and Living*. New York: Harcourt Brace and Company.

Gentry, J. Richard. 1997. *My Kid Can't Spell! Understanding and Assisting Your Child's Literacy Development*. Portsmouth, NH: Heinemann.

George, Jean Craighead. 1996. *There's a Tarantula in My Purse and 172 Other Wild Pets.* New York: HarperCollins Publishers.

Gillman, Marc. 1997. *Always Wear Clean Underwear! And Other Ways Parents Say, "I Love You."* New York: Morrow Junior Books.

Grant, Janet Millar, Barbara Heffler, and Kadri Mereweather. 1995. *Student-Led Conferences: Using Portfolios to Share Learning with Parents.* Markham, Ontario: Pembroke Publishers Ltd.

Graves, Donald H. 1994. *A Fresh Look at Writing.* Portsmouth, NH: Heinemann.

Harste, Jerome C., Kathy G. Short, and Carolyn Burke. 1988. *Creating Classrooms for Authors: The Reading-Writing Connection.* Portsmouth, NH: Heinemann.

Harwayne, Shelley. 1992. *Lasting Impressions: Weaving Literature into the Writing Workshop.* Portsmouth, NH: Heinemann.

Henkes, Kevin. 1993. *Owen.* New York: Greenwillow Books.

Hutchins, Pat. 1986. *The Doorbell Rang.* New York: Mulberry Books.

Jaspersohn, William. 1980. *How the Forest Grew.* New York: Mulberry Books.

Karp, Karen, E. Todd Brown, Linda Allen, and Candy Allen. 1998. *Feisty Females: Inspiring Girls to Think Mathematically.* Portsmouth, NH: Heinemann.

Keene, Ellin Oliver, and Susan Zimmermann. 1997. *Mosaic of Thought: Teaching Comprehension in a Reader's Workshop.* Portsmouth, NH: Heinemann.

Kohn, Alfie. 1993. *Punished by Rewards: The Trouble with Gold Stars, Incentive Plans, As, Praise, and Other Bribes.* Boston: Houghton Mifflin.

———. 1995. From Degrading to De-Grading. Speech presented at annual meeting of Association for Supervision and Curriculum Development, San Francisco, CA, March.

———. 1996. *Beyond Discipline: From Compliance to Community.* Alexandria, VA: ASCD.

Krull, Kathleen. 1994. *Lives of the Writers: Comedies, Tragedies (and What the Neighbors Thought).* New York: Harcourt Brace & Company.

Lawrence Hall of Science, Berkeley. 1982. *S.P.A.C.E.S.* Menlo Park, CA: Dale Seymour Publications.

Levine, Michael. 1994. *The Kids' Address Book.* New York: Berkley Publishing Group.

Levy, Steven. 1996. *Starting from Scratch: One Classroom Builds Its Own Classroom.* Portsmouth, NH: Heinemann.

Lewis, C. S. 1950. *The Lion, the Witch, and the Wardrobe.* New York: Macmillan.

Lowrey, Janette Sebring. 1942. *The Pokey Little Puppy.* Racine, WI: Western Publishing Co.

Lowry, Lois. 1998. *All About Sam.* Boston: Houghton Mifflin.

MacLachlan, Patricia. 1985. *Sarah, Plain and Tall.* New York: HarperCollins.

Munsch, Robert. 1985. *Mortimer.* Willowdale, Ontario: Firefly Books.

———. 1986. *Love You Forever.* Willowdale, Ontario: Firefly Books.

Namioka, Lensey. 1992. *Yang the Youngest and His Terrible Ear.* New York: Bantam Doubleday Dell Books for Young Readers.

Nathanson, Laura Walther. 1996. *The Portable Pediatrician's Guide to Kids.* New York: Harper Perennial.

NCTE. 1989. *Curriculum and Evaluation Standards for School Mathematics.* Reston, VA: The National Council of Teachers of Mathematics.

———. 1991. *Professional Standards for Teaching Mathematics.* Reston, VA: The National Council of Teachers of Mathematics.

Neilsen, Lorri. 1994. *A Stone in My Shoe: Teaching Literacy in Times of Change.* Winnipeg, Manitoba: Peguis Publishers Limited.

Newman, Judith M. 1991. *Interwoven Conversations: Learning and Teaching Through Critical Reflection.* Portsmouth, NH: Heinemann.

O'Brien, Thomas C. 1980. *Wollygoggles and Other Creatures.* New Rochelle, NY: Cuisenaire.

Ohanian, Susan. 1995. *Math at a Glance: A Month-by-Month Celebration of the Numbers Around Us.* Portsmouth, NH: Heinemann.

Palincsar, Annemarie Sullivan. 1986. "The Role of Dialogue in Providing Scaffolded Instruction." *Educational Psychologist* 21 (1&2): 73–98.

Park, Barbara. 1995. *Mick Harte Was Here.* New York: Scholastic.

Pennac, Daniel. 1994. *Better than Life.* Translated by David Homel. Toronto: Coach House.

Perry, Sarah. 1995. *If.* Venice, CA: Children's Library Press.

Peterson, Ralph. 1992. *Life in a Crowded Place: Making a Learning Community.* Portsmouth, NH: Heinemann.

Rawls, Wilson. 1961. *Where the Red Fern Grows.* New York: Bantam Books.

Reid, Jo-Anne. 1992. "Negotiating Education." In *Negotiating the Curriculum: Educating for the 21st Century,* edited by Garth Boomer, Nancy Lester, Cynthia Onore, and John Cook, 101–117. London and Bristol, PA: Falmer.

Rock, Maxine. 1998. *Totally Fun Things to Do with Your Dog.* New York: John Wiley & Sons.

Rosen, Michael J., ed. 1996. *Purr . . . Children's Book Illustrators Brag About Their Cats.* New York: Harcourt Brace & Company.

Routman, Regie. 1988. *Transitions: From Literature to Literacy.* Portsmouth, NH: Heinemann.

———. 1991. *Invitations: Changing as Teachers and Learners K–12.* Portsmouth, NH: Heinemann.

———. 1994. *The Blue Pages: Resources for Teachers.* Portsmouth, NH: Heinemann.

———. 1996. *Literacy at the Crossroads: Crucial Talk About Reading, Writing, and Other Teaching Dilemmas.* Portsmouth, NH: Heinemann.

———. 1999. *Conversations: Strategies for Teaching, Learning, and Evaluating.* Portsmouth, NH: Heinemann.

Schmar, Elizabeth. 1995. "Student Self-Assessment." In *Report Card on Report Cards: Alternatives to Consider,* edited by Tara Azwell and Elizabeth Schmar, 131–53. Portsmouth, NH: Heinemann.

Schwartz, David M. 1998. *G Is for Googol: A Math Alphabet Book*. Berkeley, CA: Tricycle Press.

Sitton, Rebecca. 1988. *Increasing Student Spelling Achievement*. Paso Robles, CA: Bureau of Education and Research.

Smith, Frank. 1988. *Joining the Literacy Club: Further Essays into Education*. Portsmouth, NH: Heinemann.

Steen, Lynn Arthur. 1989. "Teaching Mathematics for Tomorrow's World." *Educational Leadership* (September): 43–47.

Stevenson, James. 1994. *Fun No Fun*. New York: Greenwillow Books.

Strauss, Larry. 1995. *How to Reach Your Favorite Sports Star*. Chicago: Contemporary Books.

Turner, Ann. 1997. *Mississippi Mud: Three Prairie Journals*. New York: HarperCollins.

Van Cleave, Janice. 1991a. *Astronomy for Every Kid: 101 Easy Experiments That Really Work*. New York: John Wiley & Sons.

———. 1991b. *Biology for Every Kid: 101 Easy Experiments That Really Work*. New York: John Wiley & Sons.

———. 1991c. *Chemistry for Every Kid: 101 Easy Experiment That Really Work*. New York: John Wiley & Sons.

———. 1991d. *Earth Science for Every Kid: 101 Easy Experiments That Really Work*. New York: John Wiley & Sons.

———. 1991e. *Physics for Every Kid: 101 Easy Experiments That Really Work*. New York: John Wiley & Sons.

Viorst, Judith. 1972. *Alexander and the Terrible, Horrible, No Good, Very Bad Day*. New York: Macmillan Publishing.

Walmsley, Sean A. 1994. *Children Exploring Their World: Theme Teaching in Elementary School*. Portsmouth, NH: Heinemann.

Watson, Dorothy. 1996. "Welcome to Our Wonderful School: Creating a Community of Learners." In *Making a Difference: Selected Writings of Dorothy Watson*, edited by Sandra Wilde, 268–95. Portsmouth, NH: Heinemann.

Westley, Joan. 1994. *Puddle Questions: Assessing Mathematical Thinking*. Mountain View, CA: Creative Publications.

Wood, Chip. 1997. *Yardsticks: Children in the Classroom, Ages 4–14*. Greenfield, MA: Northeast Foundation for Children.

Woodruff, Elvira. 1994. *Dear Levi: Letters from the Overland Trail*. New York: Alfred A. Knopf.

Worth, Valerie. 1994. *All the Small Poems and Fourteen More*. New York: Farrar, Straus & Giroux.

Young, Sue. 1994. *Scholastic Rhyming Dictionary*. New York: Scholastic.

Zoller, Jackie French. 1990. *The Dragonling*. Boston: Little, Brown.

Index